CHRISTIN

Christina Press is a new publisher launched in 1997 to publish books by women. The founders are Ann and Edward England. Ann is a medical doctor and Edward a former literary agent and director of Hodder and Stoughton. *Precious to God* is their launch title.

'I have been involved in book publishing for thirty years,' says Edward England, 'and have not read a more vivid story of a mother's love. It is hauntingly beautiful, almost impossible to put down.'

Precious to God

Sarah Bowen

CHRISTINA PRESS
CROWBOROUGH, EAST SUSSEX

First published in Great Britain 1997

British Library Cataloguing Data
A catalogue record for this book is available
from The British Library.

ISBN 1 901387 02 X

Designed and produced by Bookprint Creative Services
P.O. Box 827, BN21 3YJ, England for
CHRISTINA PRESS LTD
Highland House, Aviemore Road
Crowborough, East Sussex, TN6 1QX.
Printed in Great Britain.

To Alice

Contents

Foreword

By Dr Corrie Weaver

It is a privilege to reinforce the messages of this enthralling book for they are illuminating and heart-warming. The insights Sarah Bowen has shared are not only for those who live with disability but also for those who consider themselves fit in body and mind.

Listening recently to a doctor speaking on the radio about the possibility of 'selecting' genes in the embryo, I was dismayed by his superficial view of the characteristics we might value in an individual and indeed of his seeming unawareness of the benefit to society which diversity offers. Physical health and good intelligence were top of his list and among others held in high esteem were strength and beauty. How sad that a person of such intellect and experience should not yet have discovered how valuable to us are those who are physically impaired, learning disabled, weak or not in the stereotype of the stars of stage and screen. Perhaps I do him an injustice for the interview was short and he might not have expressed his views comprehensively. Yet so many in our materialistic age see life in this way – that those who are 'different' do not really count. How poverty stricken such opinions make us. Is it not thrilling to see children with cerebral palsy achieving their potential among their agile peers in mainstream school; and who would not be moved by the beauty of deaf-blind people communicating by tactile sign language?

When the Apostle Paul wrote to his friends in Rome he encouraged those who were strong to bear (with) the infirmities of those who were weak. But there is a paradox here: the strong were those who tended to be in bondage to a more restrictive concept. So it is with disabled people. The 'strong' are so often those who cope not only with their impairment and all the physical and emotional energy that requires, but also have to bear with the attitudes of 'normal' folk which are frequently more handicapping. I recall asking a colleague if she had seen a television documentary on mental impairment. She had decided not to in case it would be too upsetting. The handicapped have to cope with the queasy feelings of the able-bodied!

The moving account of this family's experiences shows how they grew in strength and above all in love, not only towards their children who evoked such qualities, but towards others and towards God. This is one of the striking truths about people

with disabilities – that even the most severely limited have something to give to the rest of us, and
we do them and ourselves a great disservice by
thinking of them as always on the receiving end.
'Do not ask what we can do for them,' says Joni
Eareackson Tada, 'but what can they do for us.'
Those who have had the privilege of being close
to families with a disabled member have seen in
them the growth of qualities such as patience, ten-
derness, self-giving, encouragement and a joyful
appreciation of progress however slow. In short, a
contribution to other people's development and
growth of personality – fruit borne in the lives of
others which God puts to the account of the disabled member. Response to adversity and suffering
is a personal thing but anger is common, an almost
universal emotion somewhere along the way.
When this turns to bitterness the path ends up in
a cul de sac, leading nowhere and never to peace.
Neither can an attitude of passive resignation, nor
yet of stoicism bring peace. Amy Carmichael
expressed it well: 'In acceptance lieth peace.' Easily
said, yet those like Sarah who have proved God's
enabling in such a positive and constructive way
have truly discovered a closeness to the heart of
God.

Those who, like these splendid parents, have
plumbed the depths of grief and come through
have so much to give us. And this is true also of
those who continue to live with their limitations.
We should welcome them into our fellowships 'that
my Father's house may be full'. Which of us can
claim to be whole? Are we not all helpless and

weak? Through the apparent weakness of the Cross comes our forgiveness – and the healing of all our disabilities.

Dr Weaver is a consultant paediatrician in South Wales.

Chapter One

A warm July breeze rustles through the leaves of the beech tree under which a little girl swings high, bathed in dappled sunshine. Her laughter fills the air, mingling with the scent of roses in this rural idyll. But as the little girl jumps from her swing and runs towards me, her arms outstretched, I remember that it was not always like this.

*   *   *

Excitement, joy and apprehension are not conducive to a good night's sleep. I found myself waking up at frequent intervals to gaze at this tiny human being through the perspex sides of the hospital crib. At last, here she was. Claire Ann Bowen, born 28th May 1979; lying there, twitching slightly in her sleep and utterly defenceless. I hoped we would not fail her.

Although the birth was unplanned, after initial reservations Dick and I were delighted by the onset of parenthood. I had lost my mother in a car accident three years previously, and perhaps this subconsciously fuelled the desire for a family of my own.

We were overwhelmed with love for our daughter. Our only anxiety was that on the first day I didn't seem able to feed her properly. What sort of mother was I to be if I couldn't provide this simple, basic requirement? By day two of Claire's life, the slight twitches that I had noticed had progressed to jerky spasms, accompanied by a strange whooping noise when she inhaled.

While the hospital staff appeared to be carrying on calmly around me, I was becoming frantic with worry. Claire still hadn't taken one proper feed. In my attempts to seek reassurance from the staff, I felt I was being labelled as a neurotic young mother. Eventually an auxiliary nurse came and sat and listened to me. She watched Claire and tried to help me feed her. When we had no success, she went to fetch the ward sister. There followed a flurry of activity. For me, a blur of panic and confusion.

'Special care unit . . .'
'Paediatrician urgently . . .'
'Where can we contact your husband?'

Claire was by this time having convulsions. The drugs administered to control the fits had little effect. Someone advised me that although her life was in danger, she was not suffering. Looking down at her, unable to follow my instincts and pick her up, I found this hard to believe.

Claire was duly installed in the special care baby

unit, surrounded by tubes, beeping monitors and rustling medical uniforms. Here was my first baby, seized by something monstrous and unknown, and I could do nothing. Indeed, at that point I was superfluous to her requirements. I sat all day and night by the incubator (unless forced to bed by Sister Grice) with my hand through a side porthole, holding her tiny fingers and talking to her. It dawned on me how much more precious her life was to me than my own.

I was not a deeply religious person. I only prayed when times were troubled. Now I prayed as never before. 'Don't let her die, let her have some time, please.' Dick stayed with us, firm and strong in his conviction that she wasn't going to die. But even his certainty wavered when the hospital chaplain was called in to baptise her on day three – 30th May 1979, my twenty-second birthday.

Already this little person's character showed through: she was a fighter. There were many crises over the next few days, and the hospital staff were nothing short of brilliant. The patience and wisdom of Dr Janet Goodall (the consultant paediatrician) and Sister Grice alleviated our desperation. However, I was somewhat naive.

'If it will make any difference, we will pay for Claire to be a private patient, it doesn't matter what it costs,' I said baldly to Dr Janet.

At first she said nothing. Then, betraying no emotion, she looked calmly into my eyes and eventually said, 'I do not take private patients. Every child has the very best care that we are able to offer.'

By the end of the first week Claire's condition had stabilised. She was very sleepy all the time, due to the drugs administered to control the fits. Although not out of danger, her life appeared to be on a firmer footing. Perhaps our prayers had been answered: she had not died at two days old, and we had been given some extra time.

Dick and I needed some answers to our questions. What was the prognosis for Claire? What caused these fits? When could we take her home? How long must she take all these drugs? Phenobarbitone, phenytoin, Tegretol, diazepam. We had grown up amid great awareness of drug abuse. It was hard to reconcile ourselves to the fact that Claire might not live without them. No one was able to answer these questions to our satisfaction. Apparently it was not possible to tell why this had happened to Claire, or what the future held, at this stage. Inevitably I interrogated myself: What had I done wrong? Was it my fault? We found this 'not knowing' hard to accept. Perhaps we felt that if a label could be attached to Claire's problems or condition, then somehow this would make it understandable and acceptable.

During the first week in the special care baby unit, Claire had been so heavily sedated that she was fed by a drip. As the fits became more controlled and she was slightly less sleepy, Sister Grice suggested that I try to feed her. I had been trying to keep my milk supply going by using the hospital's human milking machine (aptly named Daisy). Dignity and motherhood do not always sit happily together! But Claire would have two half-hearted sucks and doze off again. So we had to supplement her feeds with bottles, the teat having three large holes, enabling the milk to trickle down her throat with very little effort needed on her part. Despite the efforts of Sister Grice, who dispatched Dick to the local pub to purchase supplies of Guinness, my milk dried up. 'Breast is Best' was the message from the experts; well mine certainly were not.

After two weeks in hospital with Claire, we longed to go home and be a proper family. No one understood this more than Dr Janet. So we took Claire home, still very poorly – more so than I think we realised at the time. We left the hospital, one of us cradling a precious baby and the other clutching a veritable rainbow of different coloured medicines.

The responsibility we felt was awesome. We wished we could take Sister Grice with us, but she assured us that we could phone or just arrive at the SCBU at any time of the day or night. As we said goodbye to Dr Janet, Sister Grice and all the staff, 'thank you' seemed the most inadequate thing to say to the team of people who had saved our child's life.

There we were, a family going home, thankful and hopeful, but with not an inkling of the rich tapestry into which we were all to be woven.

Chapter Two

Our home was a tiny, one-bedroomed, ground-floor flat at the back of a large white house in a country town in the midlands.

Just after Dick, Claire and I arrived home, my step-sister rolled up, complete with champagne, to celebrate Claire's home-coming. It was a warm, sunny day and we sat outside toasting Claire's health. After nine months of near-abstinence it didn't take much to send me into a coma-like sleep, leaving Dick to deal with Claire. When I eventually surfaced, Dick had fed and changed Claire, and administered all medicines with no problems. Since Claire's birth I had missed the presence of my mother. Now I realised how lucky I was to have Dick, with his easy, laid-back attitude, giving all the help and support required.

Claire slept at the foot of our bed in her carry cot. I awoke the first morning, turned to speak to Dick, but found myself addressing his feet. He had slept the wrong way round so he could monitor Claire's every breath through the night. We argued in friendly fashion about whose turn it was to feed her:

'But you did it last time, it's my turn now.'

'Oh yes, but you bathed and dressed her, so really it's my turn.'

Never, we agreed, had there been a more beautiful little baby.

Claire was so sleepy in those first weeks. It took ages to feed her as she kept dozing off after a few sucks at the bottle. She rarely woke herself for feeds. Quite often it would take over an hour to give her the medicine and required amount of milk, only for her to be sick, and then the whole process would have to be repeated. Her ability to suck was still mostly non existent, so we made large holes in the teat, enabling the milk to trickle down her throat, with the result that she suffered from wind. Claire did not put on weight as she should have done, and it was weeks before she even regained her birth weight. We were not sure if her constant sleepiness was a result of the medicines or due to brain damage. I lived in fear of her having a massive fit, fear of the unknown, fear of her dying.

On a hospital visit when Claire was a few months old, it was decided to slowly reduce the phenobarbitone and introduce other anti-convulsant drugs. It was at this point that the screaming started – a very high-pitched scream that went on and on, even sometimes when she appeared to be asleep. The only way to alleviate the screaming was to walk round and round with her, rocking her as you walked. She rarely slept for more than an hour or two at a time.

Life became a struggle: feeding, sickness, feeding, endless walking and rocking to prevent the screams. There was little distinction between day and night, and I was very tired. Dick was working for a local building firm as a bricklayer. He took time off work to help me, which didn't improve our already dubious financial state. But when you've only had a couple of hours' sleep each night, over a period of weeks stretching to months, financial considerations assume a lesser priority. Dick was a star. When I was exhausted, he would take the day off and look after Claire while I slept. What amazed us is how Claire managed to survive on such little sleep.

The hospital tried their best to balance the drugs, but it was not a straightforward business. Sometimes Claire would scream and arch her back in a bow shape, so that her head and feet nearly met. A doctor told me that it was due to cerebral irritation and she would not be feeling any pain. We found this difficult to believe; it was harrowing to watch her. Constant rocking and jogging appeared to help her, as did travelling in the car. At one point we used to joke about giving her to a long-distance lorry driver.

Initially Claire hadn't seemed very different from other babies, but as the months passed it became evident that something was very wrong. Other babies her age were showing interest in their surroundings, smiling and holding their heads up. Claire was floppy and seemingly oblivious to everything. She didn't respond to us, focus, look into our eyes or smile. I felt guilty for bringing her into the world.

On one visit to the hospital paediatric clinic, we saw a young doctor whom we hadn't met before. It was a common occurrence to see a different doctor on each visit, thus having to explain Claire's case history to a new face every time. On this occasion, having said my bit, the doctor replied that he could not see any problems and that Claire would be fine. He indicated that she might suffer from mild epilepsy, but with the medicines now available, this was nothing to worry about. My reaction was one of confusion. In my heart I knew it was not true, but I so wanted to believe him. On leaving the hospital I went straight to where Dick was working to relay the news. He was delighted to hear what the doctor had said, but as we looked at each other, it was unspoken that we knew it could not be so.

On the next visit to the hospital we saw Dr Janet. She was most concerned when I told her what the young doctor had said on our previous visit. She explained, with compassion, that his prognosis was wrong. She told us that Claire would be slow to learn and that she would need to go to a special school. It was a relief to be told what we knew to be the truth. Just how slow she would be was impossible to tell at this stage.

One of the difficulties we faced was that of finding a suitable baby-sitter for Claire. She was not easy to feed – sometimes she would choke and turn blue, which could be very disconcerting. (Administering the medicine via a small syringe often had this result.) Her screaming also worried people. Obviously we were not prepared to leave her unless we had absolute faith in a baby-sitter. Pam was a friend of ours. She was young and bubbly with no children of her own and virtually no previous experience of caring for babies. However, she was extremely good with Claire and was never fazed by her problems. She often visited us and was used to seeing Dick and me caring for Claire. So, it was duly organised for Pam to baby-sit while Dick and I went out for a meal. We had a good evening and realised how important it was for us to have time on our own away from Claire.

On returning to the flat, the first thing we noticed was that all the lights were out. In our absence there had been a power cut. The washing machine, having been halted in mid-cycle, had flooded. While testing the plunger on the syringe full of medicine, Pam had pointed it upwards and squirted the crimson liquid in a pretty pattern over the ceiling. As we paddled through the soap suds into the sitting room, Pam was having a fit of the giggles and Claire was quite unperturbed. It was the first of many occasions that Pam looked after Claire while we went out. During that period Claire spent a lot of time cross-eyed, and Pam nicknamed her Clarence, after the lion with the same habit in the old television programme *Daktari*.

Dick and I are outdoor people, but in her early days Claire most definitely was not. For some reason she totally disliked going outside and could not tolerate the slightest breeze on her face. She would alternate between holding her breath and turning blue, or arching her back in spasms and screaming. It became a major problem as Dick had the car for work during the day, so walking was the only option. I tried all sorts of different ways of solving the problem, but to no avail. So when Dick was at work with the car, we rarely went outside. Cooped up in a little flat with this screaming baby, still only sleeping for a few hours a night; with the endless round of feeding and mopping up sick, then starting again, I thought I might go insane. She didn't even seem to notice that I was there.

Surely it could not be right for Claire to be in this state? I made an earlier appointment at the hospital. We arrived at our allotted time. I was drenched after being caught in the rain at the bus-stop, then we had to wait two-and-a-half hours to be seen. Another new doctor faced me as I entered the consulting room. I went through the whole case history with her and described the difficulties Claire was having. She was not sympathetic; in fact she barely seemed to listen, never mind understand our predicament.

'I can't change her medicines without discussing it with the consultant paediatrician, who is away at the moment. You'll have to carry on and see her when she returns.'

This young doctor was obviously very busy with many patients to see. But I felt Claire's needs were being dismissed out of hand. Back home, we struggled on. Our GP and his wife were incredibly kind, but basically we felt as if we were groping our way through a thick grey fog.

At our next hospital appointment I was pleased to see Dr Janet's smiling face as we entered the consulting room. She listened carefully and heard what I was saying. Perhaps, she said, it would be a good idea to admit Claire to hospital, where she could be observed and the level of drugs checked and altered if necessary. This we duly did. As the drugs were changed, so Claire became more settled and seemingly content.

Dick and I had decided to buy our first house. It was a two-up, two-down terraced house, not far from our flat. We were thrilled to be moving into our own home. We wondered how our new neighbours would react to Claire's screaming.

At the instigation of Dr Janet, I had been taking Claire to the baby development clinic. They advised on various exercises and handling techniques which would benefit Claire. They too were unable to give me any clear idea as to Claire's future. I also took her to a local mother and baby group. The noise, however, was cacophonous and Claire spent the whole time in spasm or doing her high-pitched scream. I was aware that Claire and I were different from the other mothers and babies. I probably should have handled the situation differently, but I didn't feel welcome, more of a spectacle really. We never went back.

Just before we were due to move to our kerb-side mansion, the most wonderful thing happened. It was in the early hours of the morning. I was woken up by Claire doing her operatic impressions. Half asleep, I gathered up this very hot, puce-faced, screaming baby. I hugged her and took her into the sitting room, jogging and jiggling her as I walked. Slowly she calmed down and I sang a silly ditty to her. She appeared to be staring somewhere over my shoulder when suddenly she smiled. She was in – there was somebody there.

I woke Dick and described the smile in minute detail, but she wouldn't do it again. We celebrated with cups of tea as the dawn broke, discussing her future. Somehow that smile proved that she did have a future.

Chapter Three

Life seemed to be easier once we had moved to our new house. Claire had her own bedroom and very gradually and sporadically she was sleeping more through the night.

When Claire was born she had looked quite normal, but as the weeks and months passed, it became more evident that something was wrong. By the age of nine months she was still unable to hold her head up, and could only sit up if propped in a chair with cushions. She could make eye contact very occasionally and only for a split second. Although she appeared to feel more secure with Dick or me than anybody else, this was probably because we knew best how to handle her rather than because she recognised us. She smiled occasionally in response to high-pitched sounds and her hands were mostly clenched. She showed no interest in trying to reach out to touch any toys around her. We spent hours each day doing the exercises suggested by the physiotherapist, and bombarding her with various stimuli.

Coughs and colds were her enemies. Whereas other babies would easily shake off these common ailments, Claire would often become really ill with chest infections, necessitating periods in hospital. There were occasions when we thought she would not recover and times when we seriously questioned the quality of her life.

It was on one of our visits to the baby development clinic that the words cerebral palsy were first mentioned. On the one hand we found it helped to have a label for her condition, but on the other we had certain apprehensions about what exactly we were dealing with. In retrospect I think it was easier that we had time to let the truth dawn on us slowly, rather than have the words 'handicap', 'cerebral palsy' and 'spastic' thrown at us in the very beginning. At least that way, Claire the person came before the monster of brain damage. The handicap was secondary to the person. Although life sometimes loomed black and we were a long way from accepting the severity of Claire's handicap, we loved her dearly and still had many happy times.

My reaction was to read as much as I could about the physiology and anatomy of the brain and devour all available literature concerning cerebral palsy and epilepsy. Dick was less inclined to do this. He took each day at a time and was more able to accept Claire as she was without needing to know why.

'Why you?' a friend asked one day.

'Why not?' I replied.

Claire's fits frightened me in case she stopped

breathing and I couldn't get her to hospital in time. Although it had crossed my mind during my pregnancy that there was a possibility that our baby could be born handicapped, I had been expecting a normal baby. It was as if that baby had died and in its place was a screaming, fitting bundle whom, although I loved, I could not understand or share a relationship with. We grieved for that bouncing, happy baby who had failed to arrive. I was not sure that I could cope with what had arrived in her place. The word handicapped stuck in my throat; it was hard to say.

I felt I had to be strong, but the constant lack of sleep, cerebral scream and fits made me depressed. I didn't confide in anyone and tried to struggle on. Dick took more time off work – he was now a self-employed builder. Our financial problems added to the weight we were already carrying. I can remember castigating myself for wallowing in self-pity. I prayed, but no great revelation was forthcoming.

One day, when Claire was about fifteen months old, I was shopping in our local town when a woman approached me. She asked if I'd heard about a group which was being set up for children with special needs. The woman had recently lost a child with spina bifida and had noticed Claire. She gave me the phone number of the person responsible for initiating the group.

On our return home I studied the name scribbled on a scrap of paper – Pauline Lindsay. I pondered upon the notion of belonging to a handicapped group, but the thought of help for Claire had me dialling the number. A cheery voice answered the phone. I talked about Claire and Pauline told me about her son Andrew. He was four years old and had cerebral palsy. The two children sounded very similar, except whereas Claire was floppy, Andrew was stiff. We arranged to meet within the next few days.

Pauline's reaction to Claire on our first meeting was, 'What a beautiful little girl! Let me have a cuddle.' Pauline loved children, and after her experience with Andrew, handling Claire was second nature to her. She was very positive in her attitude which helped me tremendously. We discussed the various problems facing us. Andrew suffered from serious chest infections which threatened his life. Pauline too was accustomed to staring death in the face. We found that we also shared a similar sense of humour, which veered distinctly towards the black. No doubt people would have been horrified to hear some of the things we said. Problems reduce in size when you can laugh at them. And so began a very special friendship.

At the first meeting of the opportunity group for children with special needs, held in a local community centre, I met other mothers whose children had cerebral palsy and Down's syndrome. Far from it being a depressing experience, we actually had a lot of laughs and gained support from each other. I learnt about various allowances which were available and specialised equipment to make life easier. We arranged for professionals to come in and advise us; play therapists, occupational therapists, etc. At one group meeting, Claire and I were playing with a Jack-in-the-box which, when Jack popped up, made a fearsome screeching noise. Claire's response was immediate: her arms shot outwards and she smiled. It was the first real response she had made to a toy, so on the way home we went to a toy shop to buy her one. It became her favourite and she always smiled at the noise. When Dick came home that night he could hardly believe her reaction.

Around this time I was greatly affected by other people's reactions to Claire. Some people had no inhibitions when it came to airing their opinions: 'It would be better for you and Dick if Claire died, you can't live a normal life with her. If it was my child, I would just give her water and then she would fade and die.'

Or: 'Surely it would be better if you put her in a home. She would not know any different, and you and Dick could then have another child and start again. You do all these things for her, but what does she give back? She doesn't even know who you are.'

In a world where people are often judged and valued by academic qualifications and material success, Claire would be found sadly lacking. What was the best for her and us? Dick and I felt that we were swimming against a very strong current.

During Claire's second winter, she was very poorly many times with chest infections. We journeyed back and forth to the doctor's surgery and the hospital, often thinking that this time she would not recover. Our GP was astonished at her resilience. There were times when, having asked for his honest opinion, he would reply, 'Yes, I think she is going to die.' But she did not.

Around the time of Claire's second birthday, we reached a crisis point. Her fits were becoming more frequent and prolonged. Whether or not this was due to the anti-convulsant medicines not doing their job, or due to her condition degenerating, we did not know. As soon as she woke up she would start fitting. Light and noise would cause fits too. If we kept her in a darkened, quiet room and cuddled her, the fits and spasms would subside. Even giving her drinks and food could cause her to fit. This situation resulted in problems for me and Dick. We wanted a normal life and I could not cope with this lonely twilight existence. I was irritable and permanently tired and our marriage started to suffer.

Claire was still difficult to feed, she often choked and was sick. One morning I was feeding her breakfast cereal and she coughed, spitting the cereal straight into my face. This was a common occurrence, but on this occasion my patience snapped and I hit her. Social workers and health visitors advised us, but they did not seem to understand our predicament. We did not know where to turn for help. I felt very angry and looked for someone or something to blame for this situation, primarily myself. We were sinking in an emotional cauldron. It seemed that the only way out of this mess was either through Claire's death or to relinquish our responsibilities and put her in an institution.

Chapter Four

We could not carry on like this any more. Dr Janet listened carefully and patiently to what we had to say.

'We have decided that we want to put Claire in a home. We shall visit her, but we cannot go on any more.'

Dr Janet suggested that we leave Claire in the children's ward for a while so we could have a break. She had always made it clear that the hospital would look after Claire to give us some respite. But we were adamant. It was not a break we needed, but a permanent end to the situation. As we saw it then, it was the only way out.

So a social worker took us to look around an institution for handicapped children. We entered the Dickensian building and were enveloped by the smell of urine covered by disinfectant. There was row upon row of beds with children lying, drugged, staring at the cracked yellowing ceiling, or moaning quietly. Weird music played in the background. And we thought to send Claire to this place?

We went back to see Dr Janet. She tried to talk to us, to explain the positive side to having a handicapped child, but we would not listen to what she said. Very soon after this, a close friend was killed in an accident. It coincided with Claire's worst time.

One night Dick and I came to the decision that the quality of Claire's life was such that we wished she would die: for us, to end this nightmare, and for her, to end what we perceived to be an intolerable existence. We thought of ending her life. Without the anti-convulsants she would most likely die. So was it not playing God to keep her alive in this way?

In the next few days we took a very poorly Claire to the hospital, with the silent intention of never bringing her home again. We told ourselves that Claire would not even know any different, because she did not know who we were. Yes, we still loved her. But no, we did not want to face the future with her.

While Claire was in hospital, Dick and I decided to go away to Malta with our friend's widow and two-year-old child. We had thought that Claire would have been given a place in the institution by this time, but it was not to be. We both suspected that Dr Janet was delaying the process and we did not understand her reasons for doing so.

Our holiday was a present from my father and step-mother. We arrived in Malta during late September 1981. We were greeted by hot sunshine, beautiful clear warm sea and locals who felt an affinity with the British. It was a strange holiday though, being with our friend who had been so

34

recently widowed. Her two-year-old daughter was missing her daddy. Although she was a delightful little girl, she was very demanding and prone to temper tantrums. For the first few days Dick and I did not speak about Claire. Obviously I was concerned that she would be all right in our absence, but I tried not to think about her.

On the fourth day of our holiday I wandered off down the beach on my own. I sat on a smooth rocky shelf looking out to sea and thought of God. I had not consciously compared Claire with my friend's daughter, but I realised that all children could at times be difficult in different ways. Even though Claire was handicapped, first and foremost she was a child. Perhaps the handicap and associated problems had become a monster to be eliminated and I had somehow dismissed the child, the person, greatly in need of a mother and father to love and support her. More greatly in need than a normal child. I saw no vision of a burning bush, but as I sat there, a strength and sense of peace filled me. In that moment I knew that Dick and I would return to England and take Claire home and start again. We loved her so much. Although I was not imagining that everything would suddenly be easy, I clearly heard God's message: you will receive the special graces you need, it will be all right. All I had to do was summon up a bit of faith. I took the leaden load from my shoulders and gave it to God.

I did not relate this experience, but that evening when I spoke to Dick about Claire's future, he was completely and immediately in agreement with me. We flew home after seven days in Malta and went straight to the hospital to collect our daughter. We walked into the children's ward, where she was propped up with pillows in her bed. Dick called her and her eyes flickered towards us and she smiled.

'See, she does know who we are,' said Dick.

That evening after putting Claire to bed I phoned Pauline.

'We've changed our minds, we're not going to put Claire in a home after all.'

'Thank God for that,' she replied. 'I didn't like to tell you that it was a crazy idea all along.'

So began a new era in all our lives. This is not to say that it was all straightforward from here – there were still many blips. The hospital was excellent in offering respite care for Claire if ever we needed it. Our family also did their utmost to help and support us. From about this time God became a central focus in my life. When problems arose, which due to the severity of Claire's handicap they often did, I gave them to him and he never let me down. I also learnt that God does things in *his* time, not in *my* time. The little bit of faith that I started with grew into the greatest trust and love. Dick, although he never voiced his innermost feelings on the subject, had his own close relationship with God.

Claire was like a barometer of our new-found emotions and, gradually, she blossomed. We had not seen Dr Janet since our meeting to discuss putting Claire in an institution. Dick and I went together to see her for Claire's next hospital appointment. When our turn came, Dr Janet asked, 'And what brought about this change of heart?'

I wasn't sure what to say. If I said that I'd found God, alive and well, in Malta, Dr Janet might think that I'd gone completely mad. So I mumbled something vague to test her reaction. We looked at each other and smiled, no more words were needed. She understood because she was a devout Christian herself. Thank God for her wisdom, for now we knew why she had been stalling us in our attempt to abandon Claire.

*　　*　　*

From the age of two and a half onwards Claire's fits were more controlled. She slept much better, was more responsive and generally more content. We adjusted our lives to meet Claire's needs and I began to accept her for who she was. Our relationship with her grew and strengthened. Dick was great at devising new games to play with her. He called her Claz the Spaz; a very special bond formed between them. She developed the most infectious giggle and eventually the depression and sorrow left our lives, to be replaced by joy and an immense pride in our beautiful daughter.

'Look for the clear light of truth.' Claire had become the light of our lives. A little girl, unable to hold her head up for more than half a minute, unable to speak or sit unaided, taught us the truth about love. To give and care while expecting nothing in return – and then the miracle of finding our lives enriched beyond measure. This transformation that Claire brought to our lives was not without its effect on those around us. Watching ordinary people like Dick and me surmount our problems made others realise that they too could conquer their troubles. To face difficulties or traumas head on, and to deal with them, is in the long term much easier than running away. Most important of all, the power of God is infinite.

Claire brought out the best in the children and adults around her. It was extremely rare that we ever experienced any adverse reaction to her handicap. One such occasion happened on a sunny afternoon while we were having lunch in a pub garden. I was aware of a middle-aged woman watching me feed Claire. Eventually she walked over to where we were sitting. As I turned towards her and smiled, she said, 'If I had a child like that, I would never bring her out, it's unfair on other people.'

Before I could think of anything to say, Michael, a friend who was with us, said to the woman, 'If I had a wife like you, I would never take her out either. It would be too embarrassing for other people.'

Shortly afterwards she left. I felt sorry for her and Claire just sat in her chair smiling.

A friend of mine, Dickie, had twin girls, Rosy and Emma. They loved Claire and lavished her with attention, showing her their toys and often defrocking her while my attention was diverted. Unable to understand that she could not chew, and not wanting her to miss out on the treats, they would surreptitiously pop smarties in her mouth, causing Dickie and me the odd moment of panic in case she choked. Claire was unperturbed and thoroughly enjoyed time spent with her little friends.

Chapter Five

Claire's progress was extremely slow. We lived one day at a time and did not concern ourselves with the future. Neither did we expect any improvement in her condition. When she did make some tiny progress, it came as a great blessing. When she smiled her whole face lit up and when she giggled it was impossible not to giggle with her.

By the time she had reached her fourth birthday, Claire's incoherent babbling had begun to mean something to Dick and me. We knew when she was hungry, thirsty, uncomfortable, happy, sad, tired or that she wanted a cuddle and a chat. She loved a chat and would respond in a most social manner. As our coalman used to say, 'She'll charm the birds down from the trees, that one. Smart as paint, she is.'

She was a delight to have around and a source of great joy and love to us.

I have a fair capacity for verbosity myself, and constantly talked and sang to Claire. She would babble back, sometimes shrieking with laughter at some private joke. I was a devotee of the flip-flop shoe. Claire always knew when I was approaching due to the flip-flop noise, and she would kick her legs and make her 'I'm very pleased to see you' sounds. Our family helped us to buy a special swing for her. She adored this, and the higher we pushed her, the more she enjoyed it. She loved rough-and-tumble play with Dick, wrestling with him and being thrown high into the air. My cries of 'do be careful' were largely ignored.

During the summer of 1983 we had a wonderful holiday in Wales. A static caravan had come up for sale on a beautiful site where my family had spent holidays when we were children. The site was isolated and spartan, just a few caravans on a field adjoining a farm, within a minute's walk from the beach. There was some four-and-a-half miles of hard sand, backed by towering cliffs and headland, looking towards the lighthouse on Bardsey Island. The views were spectacular. I happened to mention to my brother, Nick, that a caravan was for sale here.

'Buy it,' he said.

'But we could only afford half of it at the most,' I replied.

'I'll pay the other half,' he responded without a second's pause.

The caravan in Wales altered our lives. We all loved the time we spent there and went as often as possible. Claire thought it was wonderful because we all lived in such close proximity. There was just one bedroom, so she had the whole double bed to herself. The local pub did not allow children inside, but the landlord was so taken with Claire that he gave her freedom of the pub for the duration of the holiday. We made new friends through Claire that year. She was offered rides on a donkey and trips on a speedboat. The latter experience truly thrilled her. She also adored going for a dip in the sea, although this had to be for a limited time as she soon became very cold. She suffered from poor circulation and her feet were nearly always chilly, which meant that she permanently wore thick woolly socks. Only on the hottest of days would she go without them. Her love of water was such that we bought her a life-jacket and would run the bath full to the brim with warm water and put her in for a soak. This she found utter bliss, and was so relaxed that she often fell asleep.

At the end of the summer we moved to a bigger terraced house with more room for Claire's ever-increasing amount of equipment.

Although Dr Janet had organised for us to receive genetic counselling, there were no clear indications as to what had caused Claire to suffer from cerebral palsy. Chromosome tests appeared normal, and there was no known history of cerebral palsy in either of our families. The experts differed in their opinions. One suggested the condition was genetic, which would result in a one-in-four chance of us having a handicapped child with each pregnancy. Another suggested that it was a one-off incident that was most unlikely to recur. There was little or no evidence to attach to either theory.

So, after much deliberation, we decided to try for another baby. Once pregnant, the ante-natal care I received was second to none. The gynaecologist, short of wrapping me in cotton wool, did all he could for me and the unborn baby. All tests and progress were completely normal. As the second pregnancy progressed, I found it increasingly difficult to bath Claire. She was becoming heavier and I was becoming lumpier. If Dick was not around to do the honours, then bending over the bath to support Claire caused backache. So I duly phoned the social services to ask for some sort of bath aid for Claire. Much visiting, assessment, form-filling and telephoning ensued. But no bath aid materialised.

At this time, it was suggested that Claire should go to the hospital for a sight test. We had a happy drive to the hospital, singing 'If you're happy and you know it clap your hands', with Claire intermittently collapsing with the giggles at her favourite bits of the song. I carried her into the hospital and we sat down to wait our turn.

The doctor carried out various tests which were not devised with a handicapped child in mind. Eventually he said, 'Of course, as you must know already, Claire is blind.' I gathered her up in my arms, clutching her closely to my grossly pregnant figure, and walked as quickly as I could back to the car. As I strapped her into her seat, I could not look at her. Had she been living in a world of darkness for these past four years? When we strung up brightly coloured toys and Christmas decorations to dangle near her hands and face, had all this been in vain? All the picture books we had shown her, had she never seen them? All the beauty in this world: skies, flowers, trees, the sea, animals, had she missed them all? How could we not have known? Should we now change the things we did, alter the way we treated her? I kept glancing at her through the driving mirror on the way home. Those beautiful blue eyes could not see. I prayed. What for, I don't know.

That afternoon I took her for a walk. Even if she could not see the bronze, red and gold of falling autumn leaves, she could hear the crunch of them under the wheels of her push-chair and feel them when I put them in her hands and closed her fists around them. She could perhaps smell the damp earth and feel the cold stream water trickling through her fingers.

As we walked, the realisation came that what the doctor had told me did not matter. She was the same Claire I had taken to hospital so happily that morning. What this doctor had said should not be allowed to destroy our peace of mind. Perhaps she did not see in the normal sense of the word. Whatever images her eyes conveyed to the brain, however the brain perceived those images, I was certain she could see something. The more I thought about our everyday life, the more evident it became that this was so.

I stopped the push-chair and knelt down in front of her. She made her 'hello, what have we stopped for' noise. I didn't speak but just watched her. She obviously knew where I was, for her hearing was very good. Then she looked into my eyes and smiled.

'You're not blind, are you Classie?'

She answered with her happy noise and giggled. So I dismissed all thoughts of total blindness and we carried on as before, showing her all there was to see, but also paying extra attention to smell, taste, touch and sound. Exactly what she saw, obviously we would never know, but she certainly could see something.

At our next appointment with Dr Janet, I related these events to her. She agreed with us wholeheartedly. Although she did not say so, I felt she thought it inappropriate for the doctor to label Claire as blind in such a quick and final manner.

It was also in 1983 that Claire started school. Marshlands School for children with learning difficulties had a special care unit for severely handicapped children. Pauline's son Andrew also went there, so we were pleased that Claire would have someone familiar with her. I accompanied her at first, but it soon became evident that she would receive good care, attention, stimulation and the necessary physiotherapy.

Of course, she could never tell us about her day, so our concerns were that much greater because we did not know what went on in our absence. To overcome this, the school had a system whereby they would write in a book about the events of each day, and we too could send any necessary messages back. Due to the nature of Claire's handicap, only those who spent a lot of time with her were able to understand her needs and interpret her methods of communication. As far as we were able to tell, she was happy there. The staff were kind and caring people who went out of their way to ensure that the children enjoyed their time there.

The downside of Claire starting school was that she caught every cough and cold going. A bug that normal children would soon shake off, often developed into nasty chest infections for Claire. She was often very poorly.

Chapter Six

On 16th November 1983, our son was born. James Richard Marshall Bowen – what a mouthful for a tiny seven-pound baby. So at the instigation of my brother, he soon became known as Jimmy.

Everything appeared fine; normal pregnancy, normal birth. We were absolutely thrilled, as were all our family and friends. On the first day home from hospital I propped Claire in an armchair and laid Jimmy on her knees. I helped her stroke and feel him with her hands and she smiled and babbled to him. She was very interested and every time he cried, she laughed. Great, we thought, at least we'll never have them both crying at the same time. How lovely it was for Claire to have a little brother, and how good for him it would be to grow up with a sister like Claire. As we had learned, his life would be richer for knowing her. Life seemed as perfect as it could possibly be. I was completely besotted with our little son.

However, in the recesses of my mind, I had a

vague niggling doubt. I couldn't put it into words and could see no reason for these feelings. I voiced them as best as I could to Dick, but felt horribly guilty, almost as if I was being a traitor to Jimmy as I did so. Dick suggested I speak to the health visitor or our GP, which I did. The health visitor's reaction was that perhaps I was suffering from post-natal depression, or that I felt as I did as a result of our experience with Claire. As I watched her examine Jimmy I was aware of her, too, avoiding some issue. When I subsequently took Jimmy to the doctor's surgery, our own GP was away and we saw another member of the practice. He assured me that nothing was wrong and that in the light of having Claire, I was bound to be concerned about the new baby. But he was fine, no need to worry. So I tried to push these fears away.

When Jimmy was only a few weeks old, Claire had a hospital appointment, so I took him along too. Dr Janet picked him up and shared in our joy. She suggested that I bring Jimmy again when Claire had her next appointment.

A few more weeks went by. My feelings of unease did not pass, in fact they increased. I could only pray. My step-brother and his wife had a son born within a few weeks of Jimmy. I noticed how much quicker he was to feed and how he was smiling and Jimmy was not. Then one cold Sunday morning in January, when Jimmy was two months old, I awoke to find him very pale and twitching. Panic filled my entire being. I phoned my father and step-mother who came immediately. My step-mother (who had a medical training) held him and said quietly, 'He's having fits. I think you should take him to the hospital quickly.'

We drove to the hospital in silence, not daring to voice our fears. Little Jimmy's face was almost white with a bluish tinge. As we carried him into the hospital I said, 'Just because he's having fits doesn't mean we must automatically presume he's going to be like Claire.'

My words were echoed by the hospital staff, who immediately launched into action, doing all they could for our son.

Within twenty-four hours the medication had the desired effect and the fits were under control. Then followed many tests to find out what was causing the fits. The doctors inserted a drip into a vein on his head. Seeing the tube entering a blob of plaster of paris stuck on his shaved head looked most disconcerting, so did the bleeping monitors surrounding the cot. We prayed. Could this really be happening? Or would we wake up from this nightmare? Jimmy lay peacefully in his cot, heavily sedated, there were no signs that he was suffering.

We had been advised not to pick him up or disturb him as this may increase any cerebral irritation. This was much against my maternal instincts. I sat by the cot talking quietly to him. Then a young doctor breezed into the room saying that she needed to take some blood for some more tests. This proved very difficult for her to achieve as she could not find a vein. After much poking about with the needle, she decided to try the vein in his neck. By this time Jimmy was screaming loudly. We had been told that he must be disturbed as little as possible – not even a cuddle was permissible, yet here was the doctor treating him like a pincushion. Filled with rage, I told the doctor to stop immediately.

'That's enough, leave him alone, the blood and the tests can wait.'

The doctor looked at me, my reaction obviously totally incomprehensible to her.

'You'd better leave the room and I'll find a nurse to help me,' she said coldly.

'Oh no, you had better leave the room and please fetch Dr Janet. I know that she will understand what I am saying.'

The doctor, whose hands were shaking, did leave the room and eventually Dr Janet appeared, bringing with her that calm and compassion with which we now associated her. The blood was taken with no fuss and Jimmy installed back in his cot.

On one of the last days in January, some seven days after Jimmy had been admitted into hospital, Dr Janet asked us to come and see her to discuss the findings of all the tests.

At home on the night before this appointment, after putting Claire to bed, I went and sat quietly in the sitting room and began to pray. After some time my mind became very calm and clear. I knew God did not choose for Claire and James to be handicapped and somehow I knew that he profoundly shared the depth of our sadness. He promised that he would give us the help we would need to cope with what lay ahead. Everything would be all right. The Holy Spirit fired and filled me, and doubts and fears were expelled. Now,

unobscured, was a deep inner core of pure peace –
a place where God is found.

Dick also knew that the prognosis for Jimmy was
not going to be good. This was his son, for whom
he had so many hopes and wishes. But drawing on
his great reserves of strength and courage, he said
to me, 'It's just going to be different from what we
imagined. If Jimmy brings half the joy that Claire
has, then everything will be fine. Don't worry, I'll
help you look after them both, even if it means
giving up my job.'

There aren't many men like Dick. The world
would be a better place if there were.

Jimmy would not be aware of what the future
held for him. He did not know that he would never
run, jump and climb as normal children do, or
grow up to be an independent adult. For the second
time, the baby we had expected had died, and in its
place was another, whom we loved nonetheless. I
thought of Claire who, despite her disabilities, had
a quality of life just as precious to her as mine was
to me. Yes, our children were different, but we
certainly knew that no less value should be placed
on their existence.

The following day we went to talk to Dr Janet.
There was no one better equipped to impart the
results and findings of all the tests relating to Jimmy's condition. Yes, it was as we thought. Jimmy
had very similar problems to Claire. Both our children were handicapped. We prayed together in a
natural, spontaneous way. Flashing through my
mind came thoughts of all the black times we had
suffered during the first two years or so of Claire's

life. In that moment I firmly decided that having been through all that with Claire, there was absolutely no need whatsoever for a repeat performance with Jimmy. No, we would crack on with life. Jimmy had his big sister to thank for his parents' much wiser and more positive attitude than that adopted first time round. Nevertheless, the knowledge that Jimmy too had cerebral palsy was a shock for us both.

It was only a couple of hours after our talk with Dr Janet that Pauline arrived at the hospital to see us. On hearing the news, she reacted in a way which served to strengthen us further. She offered no pity or sympathy.

'Let me have a cuddle. Isn't he a little darling? Oh we're going to have such fun with him. You are so lucky to have him.'

She was just the person we needed, with precisely the right attitude.

There are many times when humour has been our salvation, albeit sometimes of the black variety. As Dick and I prepared to drive home from the hospital that day, I said, 'Dick, we've got two handicapped children. When we take them out, people will think we're two social workers on a spastic outing.'

We hoped that we wouldn't be on the receiving end of people's pity. It would be an insult and a wasted, negative emotion. But we supposed it would happen and we would have to put up with it.

Dick and I knew that our families would be so sad when we told them the prognosis for Jimmy, especially our respective parents. They had been delighted by the birth of Jimmy, and now they not only had to accept a second grandchild was handicapped, but also see their children faced with another tragedy. It was hard for them all.

Later, as I held Jimmy in my arms, I remember thinking, why should I feel any differently about him now we know he's handicapped? Why should love change just because expectations had? Most strangely, I felt the beginning of a tremendous relief. We now had a reason for those feelings of unease and worry that I had experienced in those first eight weeks. Instead of secret fears, we now knew what we were up against. Our main priority was to take Jimmy home and resume our normal family life. Dr Janet understood and agreed with our wishes. So on 1st February 1984, we took Jimmy home. He was having 15mg phenobarbitone twice a day and was sleepy and floppy. He seemed quite content and did not appear to be suffering in any way, but he looked pale and poorly.

Chapter Seven

Through the Stone Opportunity Group I had met Ursula, who was a voluntary helper there. She was a trained nurse, but for various reasons she was looking for a part-time job. We arranged that she would come and help me at home for two hours, twice a week. She was a great support to us and was brilliant with Claire and Jimmy. She had two daughters of her own, who also became regular visitors to our house. Ursula and the girls were always happy to baby-sit, and with the three of them in attendance they always managed to cope when both Claire and Jimmy woke at the same time. We could never leave the children with just one baby-sitter.

Of course it was a matter of importance to us to find out why Jimmy had these problems. We spoke to various doctors. Some said that it was a matter of lightning striking twice and that there was no link between the two children's brain damage. But Dr Janet felt that there was a genetic link. Dick and I were inclined to agree with her. Their problems were very similar; it would be hard to imagine it not being a genetic disorder. We did have various tests, but all proved normal, so we were none the wiser. This did not matter to us at that point as the baby/child-care schedule in our house left not a second to consider any more children.

Although it was difficult to compare the two children, Dick and I thought that Jimmy was not as badly affected as Claire. He did not scream as much and his fits were more easily controlled than Claire's had been at that age. He slept more too. Of course, Dick and I had a better idea of what we were doing second time round.

In March, when Jimmy was four months old, Claire caught a nasty flu bug at school. She was very poorly. Our GP came out to see her and, in answer to my question, he said he thought she would not recover on this occasion. Claire had been ill many times, and at first we would take her to hospital. But as time passed, although the hospital care was very good, we came to realise that it was better for Claire to be cared for at home. When she was ill she liked to be quiet and peaceful, surrounded by familiar sounds and smells. When she was not at her best, different routines, places and people distressed her. In hospital she would often have just dozed off when a nurse would breeze into the room and wake her to take her temperature or administer medicine. This would upset Claire, thus making her feel worse not better. She was also very attached to her own bed. In view of these circumstances, the GP, Dick and I decided that we would not take Claire to hospital but look after her at home. Our GP was nothing short of brilliant in his support.

Claire was on antibiotics and we drained her chest at regular intervals. I stayed with her through the night and at one point her breathing became very shallow. I thought it might be the end. Sitting with her in the early hours of the morning, it struck me how far we had come and how much I had learned from my little daughter. She was incredibly precious to us; she loved her life. I knew she would die one day, but I prayed that it would not be now, that she would have more time.

Claire was made of strong stuff. Despite being so very ill and losing a lot of weight, within a couple of weeks she had recovered, much to everyone's amazement. Dick and I were very aware of how close to death she had been. We knew she was living on borrowed time. It was clear to us that we must make the most of each day and ensure that she had the best quality of life possible. We did not concern ourselves with what the future might hold, but lived for the present, giving her as much love and time as possible.

Dick and Claire's relationship grew from strength to strength. Dick was happily able to care for her superbly on his own. They had their own private jokes and plainly adored each other. Claire was unaware that she was any different to anyone else and was very sociable. On meeting new people, her beaming smile would dissipate any reservations they may have held. She enjoyed listening to classical music, Beethoven's piano concertos would carry her away and *Songs of Praise* on Sunday evenings would have her waving her arms in delight. She also loved a freak-out to Jimi Hendrix with her daddy.

Word quickly spread through our community that Jimmy too had cerebral palsy. Most people responded in a positive and helpful way, but there were occasions when we became the unwilling target for people's pity. This made us annoyed and indignant. Jimmy was a smashing little chap, certainly no less of a person because of his problems. We were intensely proud of both our children and pity was a fruitless, negative attitude towards our happy family. So whenever I encountered a situation loaded in this way, I prayed for the offenders to be relieved of their ignorance.

By around four to five months, Jimmy could hold his head up for a short time, but was still quite floppy. He kicked his legs, especially if he was pleased about something. He smiled occasionally too. He had a strong startle reflex which would sometimes make me nearly jump out of my skin. He also had a strong grasp reflex. This meant that if at the beginning of a morning walk (with Bumble the dog) I gave him some flowers to hold, unless I took them out of his tightly clenched fist, he would still have been clutching them at bedtime. Feeding him was a much easier task than it had been with Claire. He could swallow fairly well and didn't have the same propensity to choke as his sister had.

Jimmy, like Claire when she was a baby, didn't much like going out in a pram or push-chair, but preferred to be carried in a sling. A generous friend from the caravan site in Wales had given us a new double buggy. My steering of this buggy left much to be desired. Once I managed to hook one of the handles to the sun-tan lotion stand in our local chemist and then proceeded to drag it around the shop, causing mayhem as I went.

Initially we had put Claire and Jimmy in separate bedrooms, but at about this time we moved them in together. It was clear that they approved of this arrangement. Claire used to chat to Jimmy and although he did not respond with much babble of his own, he was definitely more content. Claire had obviously benefited from the arrival of Jimmy. She was, in her own way, developing a relationship with him. There was more going on around her and she cried less and less. People often remarked on what a happy little girl she was. Jimmy liked being near Claire and was fairly content unless there was a sudden noise or movement, which would startle him and make him cry.

One morning there was a knock on the door and who should it be but a social worker.

'Mrs Bowen, I have brought the bath aid you requested for Claire, to make bath time easier while you are pregnant.'

Any irritation I may have felt at the lengthy delay was lost to amusement. When she grew accustomed to it, Claire thoroughly enjoyed sitting under the warm shower in her bright orange deck-chair-like bath aid.

At school Claire had a physiotherapist, Mrs Unett, who was most helpful. She and Claire developed quite a friendship and Mrs Unett offered to come to our house and treat Jimmy too. We were very pleased about the friendship between Mrs Unett and Claire, primarily because this was one of the first relationships that Claire had struck on her own, without Dick or myself in evidence. We saw it as an important step in her achieving some degree of independence for herself. In this country and abroad there are various different programmes and methods of treating children with cerebral palsy. We looked into them all, including the Peto Institute in Hungary. After much deliberation and consultation, we decided against this course of action.

Life was extremely busy with Claire and Jimmy. Feeding them both and giving drinks took up a large proportion of each day. It was not possible to feed them both at the same time. Both hands were definitely necessary for each child; one to keep their head in the correct position, to prevent choking, or the liquidised food dribbling out again, and the other to spoon food in. This, combined with changing nappies, physiotherapy, playing, bathing, washing clothes, cooking and all the other household chores left little or no time for anything else. Dick more or less began to work part time, so he was always there to help in the morning and early evening, which were the busiest times. After much discussion we decided that it was just not possible (in the long term) for one person to care for both children over each twenty-four-hour period. Although financially this was not a wise decision, Dick and I knew that for the quality of our family life (and our sanity) it was the best option that his self-employed building work should take a back seat for a while.

Friends were thoughtful and kind. There was always someone calling in for a chat and to see how the children were. Cherry and her two children, Holly and Chloe used to make the most delicious cakes for us. The love and support of our friends was much appreciated.

It was clear from the attitude of various professionals, whose job it was to provide some sort of support for families with a handicapped child, that we were on completely different wave lengths to them. These professionals came expecting big problems, and when they didn't find any, either tried to invent some for us or tell us that we were suffering from some sort of denial syndrome. One young social worker, fresh and crisp from college, bursting with eager theories, said, 'If the children are all right and you are managing to cope with them, then surely your marriage must be suffering?'

My response was to say that I was sorry to disappoint him. Dick's was to show him the door. We estimated that for each one experienced, helpful professional who visited us at home, there were three duds. No doubt they all meant well.

Chapter Eight

By the time Jimmy was five months old, we were able to coax a smile from him at least once a day. He was such a good baby – chubby and simply gorgeous. Like Claire at that age, he didn't like noise or sudden movement, and he seemed to have cerebral irritation. However, the situation was resolved by giving him one hundred percent attention when he was like this. If he was carried around, cuddled or just seated quietly on my knee, he obviously felt secure and would calm down. He spent a lot of time seemingly in a world of his own, not responding to any outside stimulus. Then for a short period he would suddenly be with us, showing an interest in people or objects around him and making our day by giving us a lovely curly smile. He certainly recognised me, Dick and Claire.

When Claire arrived home from school, I would sit them next to each other and Claire would babble away to her little brother. More often than not she could elicit some sort of response from him. Our lives were different to the lives of families with normal children, in that normal children progress day by day and in so doing, their needs change. Claire and James, however, remained fundamentally the same, their progress measured on a very different scale. Our children would always need everything done for them. It could be daunting to face the prospect that, say in ten years' time, we might still be caring for them both in exactly the same way as we were then. But seen in the context of one day at a time, we were quite able to cope.

My parents sometimes had Claire and Jimmy to stay for the weekend and my step-sisters would be there to help too. We really did appreciate these breaks. However, we were aware that as Claire and Jimmy grew up, we might not always be able to rely on our family. Knowing how important it was for Dick and me to have an odd weekend to ourselves, we decided to try and find a suitable place for Jimmy and Claire to go to occasionally for respite care. The need was not imminent, but we could see that in the future it would be beneficial to us all.

On Palm Sunday, 15th April 1984, James was christened at Christchurch in Stone, where Dick and I had been married. Claire had been christened in hospital at two days old, and to ensure that she was not left out of the proceedings, the vicar blessed her and welcomed her into the family of the church. Claire smiled and had her say during the ceremony, while Jimmy took it all most seriously. It was a beautiful service, and a very special day shared with our families and friends. Both the children were in good form that day. Claire, who was becoming more and more sociable, sat in her special chair, waving her arms around, thoroughly enjoying the celebrations at home after the service. James was picked up and carried about by all our guests in turn.

As the weather became warmer, I persevered in trying to accustom Jimmy to going for walks in the push-chair. I alternated between carrying him for a while, then putting him in the seat and pushing him. Claire had eventually become used to it and I hoped he would too. It was not good for any of us to be housebound all day.

We had decided to go and spend Easter at our caravan. Initially our plan had been to spend three days there. However, the weather turned to a mini heatwave. After living in our rather dark, closed-in terraced street, the caravan seemed like paradise. The windows looked straight out to the sea, Bardsey Island and the lighthouse, bordered by the headland dotted with Lleyn sheep and yellow gorse. The peace and beauty of the place flooded everything. Jimmy was not over-impressed by the ever-present wind, but as each day passed he grew more accustomed to it. My brother, Nick and a friend spent a few days basking in the sun with us, and our three-day stay grew into nine days of glorious sunshine. Dick felt a twinge of guilt that he should be back at home working, but I thought that we should make the most of this precious time with Claire and James. Dick needed no more persuasion than that.

We returned home from Wales with renewed

strength – and how we were to need that strength over the next few months! Poor Jimmy went through an awful patch during May and June. He cried and screamed most of the time, and I did not know why. Perhaps it was due to cerebral irritation or the wrong level of medicines. Or was he in pain? To a certain extent it would pacify him if I carried him around or cuddled him; he became like a permanent attachment. It was very sad to see him unhappy like this. He hardly slept and when he woke up, the slightest noise or any bright light would upset him terribly. Dr Janet changed his drugs, but it took time to achieve the correct balance. There were times when I was so exhausted that I nearly lost my temper, but the lessons learned from our experience with Claire taught me that I must be patient.

During all this time Dick was looking after Claire, getting her up in the morning and ready for school, bathing and putting her to bed at night. They had a high old time together. The house resounded to great shrieks and hoots of laughter as they played tickling and wrestling games. As far as Claire's physiotherapy was concerned, we tried to incorporate it into daily life, in the way in which we handled and played with her, so it became second nature to us. Draining her chest was a regular necessity and mostly she quite enjoyed it. The physiotherapy must have had some benefits, but nevertheless her spine was curving more and more, and her sternum began to protrude at an alarming angle. None of these problems seemed to cause Claire any pain, but it was hard to watch as we were unable to halt the process whereby the spasms were causing her once perfect body to be twisted into deformity.

On a visit to see Liz (Claire's godmother and my greatest friend since childhood), I discussed these fears with her and showed her Claire's protruding chest bone. Liz was totally unperturbed, and she said to Claire, 'What's your mum going on about, there's nothing wrong with that, it's just your uni-boob isn't it?'

Claire giggled in response. We never worried about her uniboob again.

At the beginning of July that year (1984), we went for another weekend at the caravan. The weather was again glorious. I found it much easier to look after the children in the caravan, everything was close at hand and they were happier there – perhaps because we lived in much greater proximity to each other than at home and they felt more secure. That one weekend stretched to seven blissful weeks, with Dick travelling home to work sometimes, leaving Claire, Jimmy and myself to enjoy the sun, sea and sand. It was hard work managing on my own, but worth it just to be there.

One early evening, as Dick barbecued sausages and the children sat in their red and blue chairs, behind us the backdrop of the Welsh mountains, in front, the last boats meandering round the headland back to the harbour, he looked at me and winked.

'Great isn't it?' he said. 'How dare we be so happy. We've got two handicapped children, we should jolly well be depressed.'

We hugged and laughed, and those words became a standing joke between us.

One of the real benefits of being at the caravan was that without the demands and routine of everyday living at home, we had much more time to spend playing with Claire and Jimmy. One of Claire's favourite pastimes was to sit in her chair while I brushed her hair with a soft baby brush. She enjoyed the sensation and the attention and never grew tired or irritated by it. She was now five years old, and her capacity to understand what we were saying to her had gathered momentum. Although she was unable to talk, her range of different sounds formed the basis for a definite communication between us. She had such little control over her own life, so we made a concerted effort to try and give her some choice. 'Would you like egg or cheese?' Or, 'A red dress or blue?' Whichever word she responded to, we would take that as her preference. It was difficult to determine just how much she understood, but we gave her the benefit of the doubt. Eventually we believed she was able to exercise some degree of control and choice in her life. Our efforts to decipher her requirements were often met with gleeful shrieks – she possessed a great sense of humour.

Both Claire and James liked to touch and feel: hair, skin, clothes, animals, water, sand. I would stroke Claire's fingers gently over a piece of sandpaper and ask, 'Is this my skin?'

She would giggle so much that her whole body shook. The same reaction would be forthcoming when I helped her stroke Bumble the dog and asked, 'Is this Daddy's hair?'

Jimmy liked these sessions too, but responded in a much less obvious way. What he really enjoyed was a cuddle on our knees.

There were noises and sounds that were a source of great amusement to Claire, although neither Dick nor I really knew why. The sound of a newspaper being scrunched up, or even just the pages being turned would often result in hysterical giggling. Her response to the sound of the letter 's', as in 'Cicely's snake sneezes' would also provide a good few minutes of hilarity. So infectious was her laughter that it was impossible not to join in. Many times, even complete strangers in shops were drawn in and shared her humour.

It was a good summer for Claire, sitting or lying outside the caravan on the grass, soaking up the smell and sound of the sea, and listening to the gulls crying. Paddling in the sea was good fun, but not for too long due to poor circulation. She liked to be shown the glistening white pebbles and shells that we collected from the water's edge. Jimmy also enjoyed a quick dip in the sea. He was able to stand with support under his arms, and would curl his toes into the wet sand. At that age, nine to ten months, he did not like too much stimulation or he would become irritated and cry. Physiotherapy was most important, but sometimes the movements and exercises made him scream. I would stop immediately (against the advice of some experts) – his happiness and contentment were the first priority.

We often wondered about the world that Claire and Jimmy lived in. What exactly did they perceive? I would have liked to have seen through their eyes so we could better help and understand them.

It was sad to leave Wales and return home after so long. As I looked back to when Claire was Jimmy's age, I realised how far we had come. Bearing in mind the depth of the relationship we now shared with Claire, we looked forward to a similar blossoming with Jimmy. Experience, however, had taught us that it took time. The first two years were the most difficult for us all; we must be patient.

Chapter Nine

Over the summer Claire had grown a few inches, although she was always very small for her age. Due to the spasticity, her toes were mostly in a pointed position. (We teasingly called her Margot, as in Fonteyn.) Consequently, she no longer fitted in a normal push-chair as her toes would catch on the ground. Although I tried various methods to prevent this, we had no success. The only answer was to acquire what is called a major buggy – a wheelchair for a child. Our sole objection to this was that it would be impossible for one person to handle both push-chair and major buggy at the same time. It irked me that we wouldn't be free to go out when we chose, either to town or for a walk with Bumble, without asking someone for help.

Jimmy was now too heavy for me to carry in a sling. Carrying either one of them was not easy because they were a dead weight. I carried Jimmy on my hip, with one leg each side so as to break the spasm, but couldn't push a big buggy at the same time. Claire's legs were now quite stiff and I couldn't carry her in this way any more. Ultimately, we had no option. We would just have to make the best of a bad situation. Claire liked the major buggy. She had her own specially moulded chair which fitted onto the buggy seat: the queen on her throne. Claire returned to school in early September, brown and healthy. But after only a week or so she was ill again with a chest infection; she was still susceptible to every bug doing the rounds.

A bachelor friend called to see us one day and was amused to find me holding Claire in a sitting position on the washing machine as it ran through the spin cycle. She loved the vibrating sensation and would hoot with laughter until the cycle ended. So taken was this friend with Claire's obvious enjoyment of the proceedings, that a few days later he turned up with his Harley Davidson motor bike for her to sit on. With the engine revving away, she was in her element.

This friend had problems of his own.

'Being with Claire,' he said, 'has made me realise that I must accept my situation and come to terms with the difficulties I face instead of running away from them.'

It was around this time that Andrew's mother, Pauline and I began the battle of the nappies. Claire and Andrew were both classed as incontinent and were therefore eligible for incontinence aids supplied by the local health authority. However, the nappies that we were provided with were huge – they would have been a good fit for me, never mind Claire. They were no use whatsoever, so Pauline and I contacted the relevant department within the health authority. It took months to convince these people that our children were too small for these incontinence pads, and because of this we should not be denied a subsidised supply of nappies. Eventually, after a prolonged period of phoning and letter writing, we did succeed in securing supplies of ordinary nappies, not only for our children but for others in our area too. It was always a battle to acquire the necessary equipment for our children. Pauline, myself and other parents in similar situations had the same experience of wading through the mire of bureaucracy. We should not have had to devote such time and energy to fighting for the basics for our children at a time when we were least able to do so.

It was not a good winter for either Claire or James. They both had several severe chest infections. The fear of Claire dying always lurked nearby. Dick and I had forgotten what it was like to have an uninterrupted night's sleep. Musical beds was a nightly game – no one ever woke up in the same bed as they went to sleep in. So accustomed was I to getting up in the night that quite often I was not aware of getting out of bed, but would wake up as I bent over one of the children's beds. The following morning I could never remember how many times I had been up the night before.

The effort of physically caring for the children on a day-to-day basis was at times exhausting and extremely monotonous. But it was always worth while for the lovely little people they were. I heaped my frustrations and tiredness onto God. I envisaged him saying occasionally, 'Oh be quiet, stop moaning and get on with it.' It worked. I would laugh and make the most of life. After all, one day the children might not be here. Laughter, as I said before, is a great salvation. The closer my relationship with God became, the more I realised that he shares good humour with us.

People would often say, 'You and Dick are marvellous, the way you look after your children. I couldn't do it.'

We would answer, 'If we can do it, anyone can. We're certainly not marvellous, we just love our children.'

An experience like ours does change you though. My grandmother said to me, 'You're a much nicer person now than you used to be before you had the children.' She adored Claire and James.

Difficulties of practical caring apart, we both had much to thank our children for. Bearing in mind Claire's floppy spasticity and Andrew's stiff spasticity, on Valentine's Day that year, Claire received a card from him with a large red heart on the front. Inside was written, 'Roses are red, violets are blue, I go all stiff when I think of you.' Pauline and I joked that Andrew and Claire would get married when they were twenty-one. There was much laughter and teasing about which set of parents the happy couple would eventually live with.

There was a residential community care home for mentally and physically handicapped people near us. It was run by professional people who were kind and caring. Claire began to go and stay there for odd weekends to give Dick and me a break. Jimmy went once, but they were not really equipped to deal with babies. Claire was able to make her needs known and we knew when we went to collect her if she'd been happy or not. Jimmy was unable to do these things and so after his one visit with Claire, he never went again. Dick and I knew that as they both grew older and the years ticked by, we would need the support of respite care.

It is very clear to me now why parents of handicapped children are so protective of them and find it difficult to entrust their care to others. There was a knack to feeding and giving drinks to Claire; it was so easy to make her choke if you weren't practised at the task. If general handling was done in the wrong way it would induce spasms, and people who didn't know her very well could not interpret her efforts to communicate. Rather than think of either child suffering as a result of these situations, it was less stressful for all concerned to do it oneself. At the same time, even with a child as severely handicapped as Claire, it was most important for her to achieve as much independence as possible. Marshlands School was excellent in helping her on this score. She was very happy there and made many friends. As far as Jimmy was concerned, he just needed his mummy, daddy and sister.

Outside school Claire had lots of little friends who came to visit her or whom we went to see. She was aware of their presence and liked them to be playing around her. There wasn't a special school in our town for Claire to attend, so she had to travel some distance. The education authority provided a taxi service to school for her, Andrew and several other local children. The taxi allocated to us was driven by Albert, a very kind, funny, giant of a man, and his lovely wife, Nellie. They built up a great relationship with all the children and their parents. Claire loved them both. Albert would pick her up, chair and all, and whisk her in and out of the taxi. He even used to bring biscuits for Bumble. Nothing was too much trouble for them.

Before the Christmas holiday, Dick tried to join or weld together Jimmy's push-chair and Claire's major buggy so I would be able to take them out on my own. But try as he might, he could not find a safe way of doing it. Once, when we needed supplies from the local shop, I had an idea. I brought the wheelbarrow inside and put a thick quilt in it and then put the children side by side, propped up with cushions in the barrow. Off we went to the shop. Claire thought it a great game, but Jimmy would have appreciated a little more in the way of suspension. The three of us received some strange looks, but I was delighted to have overcome our mobility problem.

Through January and February of 1985, Claire and Jimmy suffered more chest infections. They both needed a lot of attention. Caring for them both was a struggle. Dick had to work, we needed the income, so he couldn't take time off. I desperately tried to make the children as comfortable and happy as possible, but by evening I sometimes felt brain dead. As soon as Dick arrived home from work, I would take Bumble out for a walk in the dark. It was a welcome release to get out into the countryside. One evening, as the dog and I returned from such a walk, entering the little yard to reach the back door, all I could hear was both children crying and moaning. Oh no, I thought, I can't stand any more. I can't face going in. So I opened the back door and said to Dick, 'I'm not coming in, I'm going. I've had enough.'

With that I shut the door and walked off. Seconds later, Dick was by my side, and grasping my hand he said, 'Hang on, wait for me, I'm coming with you.'

We looked at each other and started to laugh, had a hug and then went back into the house and carried on.

Occasionally we used to wonder how long we would carry on like this. Would we still be caring for Claire and James in this same way in ten years' time, following the same old routine? Then these feelings would induce guilt. For the little people they were, whom we loved so much, we would not want a life without them. It was the never-ending, practical tasks of caring which seemed so daunting, and also the fact that I was unable to care for my children adequately (long term) on my own. Prayer was the only answer for me. Through all our struggles, my relationship with God had only become deeper and stronger. Then came an experience which is as vivid today as it was when it happened.

It was late at night and I was in that dreamy state

between wakefulness and sleep. Tiredness and depression had caught me in its grip that day and I was praying for help. It was as if I was at the bottom of a well. The walls were dark and slimy and there was no way I could climb out. I was not speaking to God, but was silent in his presence. With extreme clarity, I was aware of being transported to a desert. Close to where I stood was a pyramid. A man was waiting for me. I knew he was Jesus. I walked towards the pyramid with him.

In the base of the pyramid, facing us, was a small dark opening, just big enough for me to crawl into.

'You have to go through here,' he said, pointing towards the hole.

Being somewhat claustrophobic and frightened of the dark, I was alarmed by the prospect.

'I don't want to, I can't do it,' I answered.

'Yes you can. Don't be frightened, I will be with you all the time. Even when you can't see me or hear me, I will be there. I promise.'

So I entered the tunnel, completely dark and very small, and began to crawl along it. I didn't want to do it, I felt fear and panic, but I could hear him saying, 'It's all right, I'm with you.'

Even when I couldn't hear him, I still knew he was there.

It was a long and arduous journey. Eventually I saw a pinprick of light ahead. I must keep going. The light grew brighter and stronger. My spirits lifted as I approached this light. Then, almost suddenly, I was out of the tunnel and standing on the threshold of the most beautiful, ethereal garden I had ever seen. I could hear trickling water and see grass, flowers, trees and birds in vibrant, fresh, clear colours, drenched in sunshine. But there was no sun. Such peace. Like paradise. I think it was.

Then I was aware of my bed, that I was still not asleep. I lay awake for a long time thinking about what had happened.

Chapter Ten

Due to all her chest infections, Claire's hold on life was very fragile. We were more conscious than ever that she was living on borrowed time and that we must make the very most of the time we had with our children. This served to highlight all the happy, funny moments. We were acutely aware of how much love Claire and Jimmy had brought us, and the subsequent enrichment of our lives.

Dick had always put his building work in second place to Claire and Jimmy, and although this did result in financial difficulties, he always put a far greater value on time spent with his children.

'Work will always be here and Claire and James may not,' he used to say.

I know too that he wanted to help and support me because he knew how hard it was to cope alone.

However, expenditure had risen to exceed income. So, after much discussion on how best to reverse this state of affairs, we decided among other things to tell Ursula that we could no longer afford to pay her for the four hours help in the house each week. She always worked more hours than we paid her for and was by now a good friend of the family. Although we didn't pay her much, she too depended on this extra income, and we felt pretty bad about the whole thing. It was sad for us all when we broached the subject with her, but there didn't seem any other option. Taking us all by surprise, Ursula's mother, whom we had never met, offered to pay Ursula to continue helping us each week. We were all grateful and delighted by this unexpected display of generosity.

As the winter turned to spring, Claire returned to a stronger state of health. Jimmy had his medication changed, which resulted in much better control of his fits. Thus he started to take more notice of his surroundings and to respond more. His lopsided smile would more often give way to a lovely chuckle, and although not an incessant chatterer like his sister, on occasion he made the sound 'oooo', the sound rising then falling again. He was adorable. Normal babies of eighteen months are already taking steps towards independence, whereas Jimmy was unable to sit unaided for more than a minute or so, and couldn't feed himself in any shape or form. With him being so dependent, as with Claire, the intense mother/baby bonding process had simply continued, rather than changing gradually as in the case of a normal child, developing and attaining independence.

Jimmy recognised Dick, Claire and myself and would kick his legs and smile as we approached him. It was nothing short of wonderful for us to be on the receiving end of this response. He and Claire sat in their special chairs either side of a table and were obviously aware of each other's presence. Claire would babble away and giggle with delight if she managed to elicit an 'oooo' in answer from Jimmy. Dick and I often heard the children chatting to each other in this way in the early morning.

Claire's sense of humour continued to develop. She thoroughly enjoyed the comings and goings of our friends and was frequently the instigator of unbridled hilarity. We bought an old piano for five pounds and both children liked it. They came to recognise some tunes that I played almost immediately and they both enjoyed a tinkle on it themselves.

Both Claire and James were full of love and innocence, and we knew that for the rest of their lives they would remain that way. They would never learn to be unkind, mean or bad. Dick and I had witnessed for ourselves the way in which they brought out the best in those around them, inspiring love, care, compassion and joy. In a society where so much emphasis is placed on material gain, power and academic achievement, it is too easy, through ignorance or fear, to underestimate or dismiss the priceless value of the gifts these children have to offer. By now we knew a few families with a child or teenager who was severely handicapped, and they all shared these sentiments.

It had occurred to us that had we put Claire in a home when she was a baby, how would we have felt when Jimmy was born? No doubt the emotional turmoil would have been extremely difficult to handle. How glad we were that we had come to the right decision for our family. We could not now envisage life without them both.

The spring of 1985 was beautiful, ideal for many outings and picnics. In the summer term the staff at Marshlands School took several children, including Claire, on a week's holiday to Wales. We were very lucky to have found such a good school for Claire, the staff were totally dedicated to the welfare and happiness of the children, we could not have asked for more. A lovely lady called Doris looked after Claire during the holiday. She wrote a diary recording each day's events, complete with photographs and postcards. Claire had thoroughly enjoyed herself. While Claire was away, Dick had arranged to do some work for my brother Nick, in London. So Jimmy and I went with him. We had a great few days and Jimmy especially liked his trips to Battersea Park.

We had planned to spend the summer holidays as last year. Claire, Jimmy and myself would spend the six weeks at the caravan, with Dick having three of those weeks with us. The rest of the time he was to join us at the weekends, returning home to work during the week. It was with the usual excitement that we set off for the caravan that year. I had been looking forward to it for so long, even Bumble the dog seemed to know where we were going. I needed a special large box for the children's medication, which we took with us everywhere. My friends referred to me as 'the mobile chemist'.

Both children were in good spirits and the

weather was warm and dry. The beach was very close to the caravan, but access was via a steep cliff. Dick was like a mountain goat, carrying Jimmy in his push-chair nimbly down the cliff and then doing the same for Claire. When Dick was away, there was always someone willing to give me a hand to negotiate the cliff with the children. Although the weather was warm, the sea was too cold for Claire. Her feet would turn blue within seconds of dipping in her big toe. Likewise with Jimmy, after a moment or so his teeth began to chatter. So Nick, who was often with us at the caravan, bought the children a big deep paddling pool. We filled it with warm water and, with her life-jacket on, Claire was happy to float around in it. Sometimes she was so relaxed that she almost fell asleep. Jimmy liked it too, as long as the water didn't splash his face. It was a great success.

Nick and Dick are barbecue kings; they were at it most nights. Having recently returned from a business trip abroad, Nick explained that he had a fine new method of lighting a barbecue; he assured us that it was fast and efficient. He proceeded to display his new-found technique, which proved to be somewhat too fast and efficient. Within minutes, due to the furious heat, the barbecue had collapsed and gone into a sort of meltdown. Nick and Claire were dispatched to purchase a new barbecue. On their return, Claire was sporting a new red baseball cap which she wore for the rest of the holiday.

In late August we returned home for a friend's wedding. We planned to return to Wales for a few more days before Claire went back to school. On

the first night back at home, I was vaguely aware of
Dick getting up with one of the children in the early
hours of the morning. Suddenly, Dick was shouting
for me. I had never heard or seen Dick panic before,
but by the tone of his voice, I knew something
terrible had happened. I shot into the bathroom
where Claire was sitting on Dick's knee. Her eyes
looked wild and confused and she was in great
pain.

'Her legs were crossed in spasm. I was trying to
release them, and then there was a crack . . . .'

Poor Dick's face was grey and he was shaking all
over.

I wrapped towels around her to keep her warm
and kissed her, telling her that it was all right. But I
knew that it wasn't all right and I ran downstairs to
ring our doctor. Meanwhile, we carried Claire
downstairs as gently as we could. It was obvious
that her leg (the femur) was broken. The doctor on
call was from a different practice. He had never met
Claire before, but he was marvellous. We carefully
made a splint to hold the leg in place before driving
to the hospital. We telephoned Ursula, who was
round at our house within minutes, accompanied
by her two daughters, to look after Jimmy while
Dick and I took Claire to the casualty department.

Little Claire was suffering and she could not
understand why. All I could do was cradle her on
the back seat, keeping her leg as still as possible,
talking quietly to her and kissing her hand, which
she always loved. The doctor had already telephoned the hospital to tell them that we were on
our way. As soon as we arrived, they leapt into

action. A nurse gave Claire some diazepam to keep her calm. Dick had been explaining to another nurse exactly what had happened. Then another member of the staff asked to have a word with me. Slowly, with increasing horror, it dawned on me what this person was saying. They thought Dick had been violent towards Claire and had broken her leg. Dick, who obviously felt utterly terrible about what had happened, did not deserve this. He looked desperate. I understand that hospitals must ask questions under these circumstances, but that did not quell the rise of anger that I felt. No father loved a daughter more than Dick loved Claire.

We needed to be with Claire, not wasting time dealing with these accusations. I suggested that the hospital contacted Dr Janet – she would tell them what sort of parents we were. I told the doctor on duty, 'If we were the sort of people who abused our children, then I assure you, Claire would have died long ago.'

He looked bemused.

Dick and I then went with Claire to have her leg X-rayed. The diazepam had made her drowsy. She kept drifting off to sleep for a few minutes, then she would wake and in that split second give me the beginnings of a beaming smile before the dreadful pain registered and her face screwed up in a way I had never seen before. It was simply awful. Once the doctor on duty had examined the X-rays and diagnosed a fractured femur, the attitude of the staff changed towards us. The doctor said that now he had more information, he realised that Dick was not to blame. After studying the X-rays, it was perhaps surprising that Claire had not broken any bones previously. Dick was relieved to be no longer under suspicion. Even though all concerned assured him that it was not his fault but an unfortunate accident, he still felt guilty and blamed himself. Meanwhile the doctors decided that Claire's leg should be put in full plaster and then in traction.

Knowing as I did, the positions and situations which triggered off Claire's spasms, I was concerned as to the outcome of this course of action. I voiced my fears immediately. Sadly, but not surprisingly, the doctor did not listen. I tried to explain that the treatment they had decided on may be fine for a normal child, but it would be wrong for Claire. What does it matter I asked, if the bone does not heal precisely as it should. After all, she will never walk. I stressed that her comfort must come first. The doctor looked nonplussed and asked what qualifications I had to dismiss his recommended treatment, and then suggested that I let him continue with his job. I understood his predicament, but why could he not see that Claire was not a normal case of a child with a fractured femur?

Claire was very distressed, the pain-killers and diazepam administered at frequent intervals did little to alleviate her suffering. Her leg was duly put in plaster and she was taken to a ward where she was put up on blocks and traction.

Chapter Eleven

Dick and I decided that he should go home to look after Jimmy and I would stay with Claire. All that day Claire's condition deteriorated. To be lying on her back, with her broken leg stretched out in front of her, was the worst position for inducing the spasms, which seemed to be racking her little body with increasing frequency. More doses of diazepam had little or no effect.

By early evening I decided to go home to have a quick shower and collect various things that Claire and I might need for our stay. The journey home took about fifteen minutes. As I walked through our front door, the phone was ringing. It was the hospital.

'Please could you return immediately Mrs Bowen. Claire is screaming, and we don't know what to do with her.'

As the ward sister spoke, I could hear Claire in the background; a scream of pain and desperation. I dropped the phone and belted back to the hospital.

As I entered the ward, Claire heard my flip-flops on the hard floor. She paused in her screaming, I spoke to her and gently gathered the top half of her body into my arms. She visibly relaxed and calmed down a little. All I could do for her was to kiss and hug her, but I couldn't stop her suffering and take the pain away. As the evening wore on, her spasms grew worse and more frequent. I had a horrible feeling that she might die. 'Dear God, please don't let her die like this, please do something. We haven't come this far for her to die in this way.' Thoughts like swelling waves crashed through my mind. She did not understand what was happening, her face registered confusion, fear and pain. How would Dick feel if she died like this?

I held her little hands, they were so soft. I used to tease her about her hands – so soft because they had never done a job in their lives. She would giggle in delight. I asked the ward sister to phone Dr Janet, but they said no, this was not her ward, and she would not be able to do any more than they were doing.

It was a long, long night. Claire was exhausted, but because of the spasms and discomfort she was unable to do more than doze for a few minutes at a time. At about one o'clock in the morning, her breathing became very shallow and the spasms gave way to a fully blown fit. Yet more diazepam was administered but it had no significant effect. The staff on the ward were obviously at a complete loss as to what to do next. Then, about one hour later, Claire suffered a respiratory arrest or a severe fit, no one was sure which. I thought she had died.

Then, after what seemed an age, she took another breath. The cardiac arrest team surrounded her bed. No one seemed to know what to do.

'Please, please, telephone Dr Janet and ask her to come in,' I begged.

'We can't do that now,' the sister answered. 'But we'll try and contact her in the morning.'

'But it may be too late by then, please do it now.' My voice was sheathed in panic.

The cardiac arrest team looked from Claire, to me, to the sister. No one spoke.

Eventually, unable to cope with what my daughter was going through any longer, and desperate to save her from any more pain and suffering, I screamed, 'Phone Dr Janet now.'

I was vaguely aware of staff conferring. Then the sister nodded at me.

'I'll just go and contact her now.'

Relief eased my panic.

'It's all right Classie, Dr Janet will come, she will make it better.'

I don't know what I expected Dr Janet to do, but I had such faith and trust in her, I knew she would not let us down.

At around three o'clock, the doors at the end of the ward opened quietly. There, framed by the corridor lights, was a smiling Dr Janet. In the presence of her calm, dignified manner, the air of desperation evaporated. She spoke quietly to Claire and then to the ward sister. Within minutes she had assessed the situation and decided on the best course of action.

Immediately the blocks and traction were

removed and Dr Janet asked for Claire to be given morphine. The sister explained that it would be difficult to obtain morphine until later that morning. Dr Janet was undeterred and disappeared into the office to use the telephone. Some five or ten minutes later the morphine arrived, and Claire was given her first dose. The transformation was immediate and appeared miraculous. Claire, from being in the grip of such pain, her body twisted by spasms, suddenly relaxed and a beautiful, peaceful smile spread across her face. I witnessed God working through Dr Janet. Claire's life was saved. Words cannot convey the depth of our gratitude.

Arrangements were swiftly made to move Claire to Dr Janet's own ward where the staff knew and understood her special needs. Claire, with the morphine eradicating all pain and discomfort, was in a state of blissful contentment. The full plaster was removed from her leg and a smaller splint-type support fitted instead so that she could still bend her leg at the knee.

After a few days we were allowed home. Dr Janet always understood our desire to return home as soon as possible. Dick had been doing some building work for an orthopaedic consultant who lived near us. As soon as Dick told him about Claire, he immediately offered to come and see her at home to save us having to take her back to out-patients. He was very kind and came several times to check on her progress and to show Dick how to make replacement splints.

When the time was right, we weaned Claire off

the morphine. The withdrawal did have some adverse side effects, but only for a short time. In my humble opinion, the benefits of this drug, in a situation like Claire's, cannot be overstated.

Chapter Twelve

It was two weeks since Claire had broken her leg and the August bank holiday weekend was imminent. We decided to take the children to the caravan. It would do Claire good after all she had been through. The weather forecast was promising and Claire was becoming her old self again. Obviously we were extremely careful with her. The leg was healing well, with a slightly thickened, bow effect to the femur.

Years before, my mother had bought a foal for me from the farm where our caravan was sited. I had been told that another foal had been born nearby. We took Claire and James to see the little creature. Dick and I dreamed of the possibility of buying it. Considering that we lived in a terraced house with a small garden, it was hardly a practical idea, but the seed was sown. Having been lucky enough to live in the country and to have had a horse before I was married, I missed that way of life. With Claire and James dominating my days, I knew that having a horse again would be a sure safeguard for my sanity. But financially it was out of the question.

Not long after returning from Wales, I was talking to Nick on the phone, telling him about the foal in Wales.

'If you would like a horse, I will buy you one,' he announced.

Only on rare occasions have I been speechless with amazement, and this was one of them. As Nick wasn't there in person, I hugged the phone instead. What a generous brother I had.

Discussions with Dick ensued. He was nearly as enthusiastic as I was and quite happy with the idea. Now I had to find a field to keep the proposed pony in. A family friend lived within walking distance of our house and they had some ponies and land. I tentatively enquired if they might have room for another. Yes, came the reply – and for a very reasonable weekly rent. I received an attendance allowance from the state for Claire so that I could afford to pay someone to come in and help me. It was enough to cover perhaps one night a week. After much thought, we decided that although a pony did not fall into the latter category, it would indeed bring an added dimension to our lives (mostly mine) in other ways. So we began our search for a pony that could live out in all weathers and would not be too expensive to keep.

Enter Harriet; a 14.2 hands, pretty bay mare, very strong with a naughty streak running thickly through her veins.

'Classie and Jimmy, meet your new nanny, Harriet.'

'Aaaa,' said Claire.

'Oooo,' said Jimmy.

They were both intrigued, and showed great interest in this furry beast. Looking back, I can't imagine how I envisaged I would find the time to look after everyone. But I was undaunted and utterly thrilled to have a pony again.

The first ride I had, Harriet and I trotted off, with Dick, Claire and Jimmy following at a safe distance in the car. I felt that my whole life had changed for the better. Once Claire had gone back to school, I would put Jimmy in his push-chair and take him to Harriet's field. He enjoyed being there, stroking the other little ponies and having a sit on them. He was happy to be in the middle of all the activity, watching and listening. In the early evenings when Dick came home, I would nip off for a quick ride. Dick never complained and I was very aware of how fortunate I was. I took Bumble with me on these rides, and she loved it too.

Claire, because of the spasticity in her legs, could not sit on a horse astride. After breaking her leg, we were very careful. However, she could manage to sit side-saddle – Queen Claire, trooping the colour. With all the physical aspects of caring for Claire and Jimmy, added to the riding and looking after Harriet, I now had biceps that would have been the envy of Fatima Whitbread.

Towards the end of September we had an Indian summer. Jimmy spent the days around the stables with me and Harriet, or in the garden. He loved the swing and smiled his special curly smile as I pushed him. After Claire being at home for the long summer holiday, I appreciated the extra time I could spend with Jimmy. He was much more settled now, his fits seemed under control and he was becoming a real character in his own right, as if out of a mist a clearer picture was emerging. He was such a sweet, loving little person.

On Saturday 16th November 1985, we celebrated his second birthday. He liked all the wrapping paper from his presents and we sang 'Happy Birthday' to him throughout the day, with Claire performing her operatic version. Jimmy knew something special was happening and paid attention to the proceedings, kicking his legs, smiling and showing his appreciation with a few 'oooo's.

That night, when both children were asleep in bed, Dick said, 'He's two years old, the first two years are the most difficult, we're through the worst.'

We agreed; there was much to look forward to. The next Saturday there was a fête at Marshlands School and we all went along. Several people whom Dick and I didn't know came up and said hello to Claire. Her response was friendly and social. Again we were delighted to see evidence of her ability to form relationships with other people. The school staff made a point of talking to Jimmy. 'I can't wait to have him here. Isn't he a sweetheart, and doesn't he look well?' one of the teachers commented. We bought a Christmas tree decoration – Christmas was only a month away.

Chapter Thirteen

We woke late the following morning. The silence in the house was broken by Claire's voice calling to Jimmy. Odd that there was no response from him. I hurried along the landing into their bedroom. Jimmy's eyes were closed. I knew instantly that he was not asleep, but that he had gone. At that stage, the word 'dead' did not enter my head, just that he had 'gone'. Then Dick was behind me. I picked Jimmy up, so gently; but we knew it was too late. Jimmy was dead.

We phoned the doctor, who was the same kind and sensitive man who had come out in the middle of the night when Claire had broken her leg. As if we had some bizarre hope that he might be able to bring Jimmy back. I hugged my son's little body to me, and prayed. I was numb, suspended, on the crest of emptiness. Being able to hold him was so important. Although he had gone, his body remained, like a half-way stage, while we grappled with this reality. This secret awesome death, that held no fear; in the face of such stark reality, we are helpless.

The police arrived some time later; they have to be called out when someone dies unexpectedly at home. One of them, a young man with a small son of his own, was compassionate. The other, an older policeman, was cold and aggressive. My father, who had arrived shortly before the police, dealt with him. This policeman asked for police photographers to be sent, and he kept asking me questions. I understood that he had a job to do, that the police must protect children and be certain that there was no foul play. Nevertheless, I was appalled by his behaviour.

When the police photographers arrived, I took them upstairs where Jimmy was lying in his bed. They silently looked around and then one of them took my hand, 'Sorry love, we shouldn't be here. There was no need for us to be called out, we won't be taking any photographs.'

With that they left, followed shortly by the horrible policeman.

We took our time to say goodbye to Jimmy. Claire gave him a kiss. She knew something was wrong, but she was not aware that he wouldn't be coming back. All the same, we explained what was happening; you could not be certain of just how much she understood.

Those last few minutes with what remained of Jimmy were infinitely precious. I carried him downstairs for the last time and against all my instincts, handed him over to the undertaker. Dick and my father were standing close by, I will never forget the look on their faces. As the undertaker drew up the zip of the black body bag, something icy clawed at my insides and ripped them out. Part of me had died too.

When everyone had left the house, I sat on my own in the sitting room, shocked. Dick brought Claire in to see me, his face was grey but he was so strong. I held Claire's soft hands and she gave me her beautiful smile. We had to go on, she needed us.

There were so many unanswered questions. God was with us, Jimmy was with God. We couldn't let him go, but had to. It was as if our lives had been suddenly frozen in mid-motion. If only time would stop, because every passing second took us farther away from Jimmy. Our family and friends gathered around us, offering comfort and support. Dick and I drank a whole bottle of whisky that night, but were icily sober. Claire missed Jimmy. In her own way, she grieved too.

On the morning of Jimmy's funeral we awoke to a white world. The snow was several inches thick. It had snowed on our wedding day too. After breakfast I went to give Harriet some hay, and leaned on the gate, watching her while she ate. There was no Jimmy in his push-chair now. Perhaps he was with my mother. I hoped so. There was never any doubt in our minds that God would take care of Jimmy, and Claire, Dick and me. But I thought smiles and laughter had left my life for ever, and that no time would ever be sufficient to accommodate our grief.

The funeral service was beautiful, the coffin so

tiny. The love of God, each other, our family and friends saw us through that day. A few days later, Claire brought a painting home from school that a teacher had helped her to paint. It was a rainbow, the colours as bright and bold as its message of hope.

There were unanswered questions surrounding Jimmy's death. The GP described it as a cot death. He had not appeared to be ill, although he had been snuffly when I was up with him in the middle of his last night. But I had not noticed anything out of the ordinary. Perhaps I should have done, I will never know. Dr Janet let us read the post-mortem report, which recorded the cause of death as bronchopneumonia. The thought of Jimmy having a post-mortem upset us both, but Dr Janet's words helped a great deal: 'Remember that his body is only the house in which he lived.'

I shall always wonder if I could have done anything had I been with him. Did he know what was happening? Did he want his mummy, but she wasn't there? I can only have faith and trust in God that he would not have allowed Jimmy to suffer. There followed a grey, bleak time. When Claire was at school, I missed Jimmy the most. Thank God for Harriet, because I spent my days with her and I felt that it was no coincidence that she had come into our lives when she did.

When a handicapped child dies, perhaps it is inevitable that some people adopt the attitude that 'it's for the best', or 'it's a blessing in disguise'. We found it very hurtful. It is not so simple to sit in judgement on the quality of life of another. His life was as precious to him as my life was to me. Just because his expectations and potential were different from the norm, did this make his life a less viable proposition? As the person most able to speak for Jimmy, I am compelled to answer, 'I think not.' He had two years and one week; such a short little life. Four weeks after his death, it was Christmas. It was a sad time for us, but Claire was a great solace; we appreciated her so much.

Chapter Fourteen

Now that we only had Claire to look after, it all seemed rather a doddle. She was such a happy, outgoing, easy little soul and her sense of humour filled us with delight. Not so long ago, I had thought I would never laugh again, but Claire made sure that I did. We knew that the experience we had just been through with Jimmy was, at some unknown point, going to repeat itself with Claire. We renewed our pledge to make the most of every moment we had together.

It didn't take much to make Claire happy, just our love and our time. Material possessions were of little consequence to her. We went for lots of walks with Bumble, bumping the buggy over fields, bogs and streams. Claire giggling and giving me verbal encouragement as I puffed my way up the hills, sounding like a pair of old bellows. Dick could now devote himself more to his building work and business was slowly picking up.

My brother Nick became engaged to Jill. On our

first meeting, it was as if we had known each other for years. Although she had little previous contact with children and was a high-flying business woman, she established an immediate rapport with Claire. Jill travelled the globe on business, and Claire soon built up an impressive collection of T-shirts from various countries. The favourite was a white one from Antigua with 'no problem' written in large blue letters on the front. It was Dick's catch phrase of the moment. She wore that T-shirt on a visit to the dentist one day with Dick. The 'no problem' certainly didn't apply to the dentist – Claire accidentally nearly bit her finger off!

I had considered finding a part-time job to fit in with Claire's school hours, but she had so much time off school with colds, coughs and chest infections that it wasn't a feasible proposition. So I was lucky to feel justified in staying at home, doing the household chores and the administration of Dick's business at double speed, to enable me to spend the remainder of each day with Harriet.

Through a friend, I became involved with riding for the disabled. Children from a local special school, with varying degrees of handicap, gathered each week at a nearby riding school. It was evident even to the most untrained eye that the children benefited enormously from these sessions. Week by week they gained in confidence and ability. When riding a pony, children who were unable to walk were, for the first time, in control of when and where they went. Without the children being aware, it was also a useful physiotherapy session. I am certain that encouraging contact between handicapped children and animals can be a factor in helping these children to fulfil their potential.

Claire was now seven years old. She still couldn't hold her head up for very long, but she used her hands more. We still dangled toys or shiny Christmas decorations at strategic positions around the house, and she played with them for hours. She was still unable to feed herself, but looking after her had become second nature to Dick and me. We just got on with it and rarely thought any more about it. Claire still woke up often in the night, but we had grown accustomed to it and it was not a problem. Having lost Jimmy, we felt very fortunate that Claire was still with us; the ongoing caring and broken nights seemed a tiny price to pay.

In retrospect, I had not been much more than a child myself when Claire was born. In some ways it was as if we had grown up together. She was the most loving little person and the love we shared was so special – love that grew from giving, caring and not expecting anything back in return. The rewards from our relationship with Claire were immense, nothing could ever change that, not even death. She and Jimmy had taught their parents the true meaning of the word love.

Dick and I were also aware that despite the severity of her physical and mental handicap, she understood a lot of what we said to her, and we recognised an inner wisdom in her. Perhaps this stemmed from her simplicity and innocence. A teacher to whom she was particularly close noticed this too. Occasionally when we met new people

now, it was evident that at first they felt sorry for
Claire. This made me smile inside because she was
probably happier and more at peace with herself
than they would ever be.

Claire and I spent the long summer holidays of
1986 at the caravan again, with Dick joining us for
three weeks and every weekend. Claire enjoyed her
boating trips with friends and dipped her toes in
the sea. She still basked in the honour of being the
only child allowed in the local pub. One day, Dick,
myself and some friends were enjoying some surf-
ing. The bay was excellent for this sport. We had
left Claire at the sea's edge, sitting in her buggy.
Bumble adored the sea and always came in with us.
After a while, we noticed Bumble barking madly
and circling round Claire. Dick and I waded
quickly to the shore to see what was wrong. The
tide had come in more quickly than we thought
and the waves were lapping around Claire's ankles.
Claire thought it was a hoot, but Bumble was
clearly unimpressed with our oversight – she was
always very protective of Claire.

We had a favourite place by the cliff where
Claire, Jimmy and I used to go and sit, overlooking
the beach and the sea. That summer Claire and I
spent many hours there. Sometimes I'd pick her up
and we would dance; it made her shriek with
delight and laugh until her whole body shook. It
was close by this spot that we decided to scatter
Jimmy's ashes. A place of beauty and peace where
the four of us had shared much happiness.

On the drive back home from Wales that year, the
journey, due to the heavy traffic, took longer than

usual. Claire was hungry and would soon need her medication, and with some sixty miles yet to go, I suggested to Dick that he put his foot down a little. A few miles further on we whizzed through a police speed trap, subsequently pulling into a lay-by, as directed by a frantically gesticulating policeman. As the car stopped, Claire had a spasm, and at precisely the second that the policeman's face peered through the open car window, Claire let out a long moan. The policeman looked at her in confusion,

'What's wrong?' he asked.

'We're hurrying to get home, she's handicapped and needs her anti-convulsant medicine,' I replied.

The policeman leapt away from the car, flung out his arm to point in the direction we were heading and shouted, 'Drive on.'

Needless to say, we instantly obeyed his orders and as the car gained speed, Claire's spasm turned to giggles. Dick looked at her through the rear-view driving mirror. 'Classie Bowen,' he said, 'you're beyond the law.'

During the winter of 1986, Claire's health deteriorated again. The curvature of her spine resulted in her lungs and other internal organs becoming squashed. She had several serious chest infections and when the prescribed antibiotics seemed to be having no effect, we took her into hospital. Although Dr Janet and her team gave her the best possible care and attention, Claire found the whole hospital experience stressful. As always when she was poorly, she was much happier at home in familiar surroundings. Again, there were times when we didn't think she would recover, but she proved us wrong. No sooner had the face of death retreated, than Dick would be aeroplaning Claire round the house again and throwing her up in the air, both of them laughing and shouting as he caught her.

The first anniversary of Jimmy's birthday and his death a week later was a poignant time. We missed him so much. We began to contemplate the possibility of having a third child. If the problem with Claire and Jimmy was genetic, then could we take this risk? The odds would be one in four (with each pregnancy) that the baby would have cerebral palsy. Or had lightning struck twice and would a third child be unaffected?

We considered adoption or fostering an older child with a view to adoption. Our discussions also centred around AID (artificial insemination by donor). For many reasons we eventually dismissed these options and tried to accept the fact that we would not have any more children. I gave away all the baby clothes and equipment. No matter how much we loved Claire and James, it did not stop Dick and I hoping that one day we might have a normal child. Claire would love a brother or sister too, but I thought it was a pipe dream and something that was just not going to happen for our family.

There are always people better off or worse off than oneself. We had a friend who had been through many difficulties. He was kind, bright and intelligent. But over a period of time he became very depressed and turned to drugs. What started as something to help him through the bad days, eventually became a full-blown heroin addiction. We were very concerned, but nothing anyone did or said seemed to help this lost and lonely person. He disappeared and we didn't see him for some time. Then one evening he turned up on our door-step looking fit, healthy and with a smile on his face. Over a cup of coffee he told me, 'It was know-ing Claire that helped change everything. I realised that I was wasting my life. I thought of Claire with all her problems and I felt ashamed. That was my turning point.'

And some people are of the opinion that those of us suffering from severe handicaps put nothing back into society!

Chapter Fifteen

Nick and Jill were now married and living in Kent. We often travelled down to see them. Claire always enjoyed her time there. She had her own bedroom, decorated in pink, with Jill's childhood teddies to keep her company.

Claire had recently had a new chair, designed along the lines of a car seat, but specially moulded to her shape. This chair could be fixed in her buggy, attached to a wooden dining chair, used as a car seat or fixed into a mobile metal frame. It proved to be a very useful piece of equipment, although extraordinarily expensive. In fact, most specially designed aids for the disabled are extremely costly. I know families who have really had to struggle to provide such necessary equipment, despite the existence of special government or national health service grants and charities to help fund these basics.

Claire was still happy at school and we had recently received her annual review, the equivalent of a school report. It is with great pride that I quote the following extract:

> Claire Bowen is an absolute charmer, who is able, despite her severe physical handicap, to wind everyone around her little finger with her winning ways and smiling face.
>
> She is popular with children and staff alike and enjoys nothing more than a good conversation with them, looking directly at them, smiling and vocalising, looking a little worried and quivering her lip if she is being told off (usually 'Claire don't spasm'). She doggedly refuses to allow anything past her lips that she doesn't like or want during tasting sessions and mealtimes, and will play games with a new person giving her lunch, by hiding her mouth in the right side of her chair while chuckling.
>
> She is a delightful, well-adjusted, sociable little girl.

1987 was, apart from the inevitable chest infections, the happiest year yet for Claire. Life for her and with her had certainly become easier and easier as time passed. We were often out and about, visiting friends and nipping down to Kent to stay with Nick and Jill. Work for Dick was going well too. One day, Claire was in her special chair at the table and I was sitting close by, writing. She stretched out her arm and laid her hand gently on my head and stroked my hair. I looked into her eyes and she smiled; her gift of love and joy will always be with us.

Claire went on holiday with the school to Criccieth, North Wales, and by all accounts, had a marvellous time. We spent our summer holiday, as usual, at the caravan. The grief for Jimmy had formed a scab, but then something unexpected would tear it off, revealing the raw wound. However, the days spent with Dick, Claire and Bumble by the sea were healing. I can remember the smell of coconut sun-tan oil and hear Claire's bursts of laughter. It was one of her best summers.

Inevitably there were occasions when we contemplated Claire's death. Sometimes we could talk about it quite rationally, but at other times the thought seemed impossible to handle. We could only pass these fears to God and know that he would take care of us all. I remember lying in bed with Claire early one morning, listening to the sea crashing against the stones below the cliff at high tide. She had been close to death more times than I could recall. Perhaps she would still be here at fifteen years old, sixteen, seventeen? But she was with us *now*, and I hugged her bony body and told her how very much we loved her.

Again, Dick and I considered having another baby. Claire so enjoyed the company of her many friends, especially that of my little god-daughter, Natalie. We knew she would dearly love another brother or sister. However, we were most aware of the high risk of having another handicapped child. So we put the idea out of our minds.

We spent part of Christmas that year in Kent with Nick and Jill. Jill had decorated the Christmas tree with great care and style. She did not utter one word of reproach when Claire rolled under the tree and proceeded to bash away at the glittering tinsel and shiny baubles. It was Claire's favourite Christmas activity. Consequently, all the pine needles fell off the tree and well before New Year's Eve, the poor tree was totally bald. After a wonderful Christmas and New Year, we returned home.

In late January 1988, Claire caught another cold which she could not shake off. She was well enough to go to school to celebrate Red Nose Day (comic relief). As she was intensely irritated by the standard red nose, one of the teachers put lipstick on her nose instead, so she could not be accused of being a party pooper. Claire apparently enjoyed all the fun and games, and was most impressed by the musical concert given by the peripatetic music teachers. The cold developed into a chest infection and the prescribed antibiotics did not seem to be having the desired effect. We had arranged for me and Claire to go and stay with Nick and Jill, with Dick joining us for the weekend. I toyed with the idea of cancelling the trip until Claire had recovered, but eventually decided to go. Jill, who was up in the midlands on business, came to pick us up. Although Claire was very tired, she seemed all right on the journey down to Kent. I was well stocked with a new antibiotic, which hopefully would knock the latest chest infection on the head.

By the time Dick joined us in Kent on the following Friday evening, Claire was very ill. She was so tired, her body gripped by an exhaustion that sleep would not ease. Dick and I discussed every option and decided against taking her to hospital. The strange environment would do her more harm than good. We did not want her to suffer from tubes being poked down her nose, injections or drips. We loved her too much to do that to her.

Some months previously, Dick and I had said to each other, 'It's as if she's slowly dying.' Those words were now in the forefront of my mind.

Claire spent most of Saturday with Dick in the warm sitting room. She absolutely adored her daddy. We did what we could to make her comfortable and cocooned her in tender loving care. The memories of that day are striking in their clarity. Afternoon darkened to early evening. She did not appear to be suffering any pain at all, but was worn out and very weak. Even as her life was ebbing away, she still managed to give me one of her beautiful smiles. I sat on the sofa with Claire in my arms and Dick by our side. It was calm and peaceful. We prayed.

When our daughter was expected to die at two days old, I had pleaded with God to give us some time with her. She was now eight and three-quarter years old. We had been given a lot of time. Now we knew that we had to let her go. Amid this beautiful, awesome tranquility, Claire's soul slipped from the body I held, into the arms of God. At some point, I heard the news on the television in another room. How strange that while our world had stopped, everyone else was carrying on about their business as usual. As when Jimmy died, I wished I could halt the passing of time, because every tick of the clock took Claire farther away from us.

Chapter Sixteen

Dick had a vivid dream that night. He saw Claire, across a street, through a window. She was sitting on my mother's knee, still the Claire we knew, but not handicapped any more, and she smiled and waved at him. We knew she was free of her crippled body, we could not wish her back. Some intangible part of each of us died with Claire, perhaps to be found when we meet again. There was a large cupboard in Nick and Jill's kitchen. I remember wanting to get in it, to lock the door and hide there indefinitely. For Nick and Jill, in whose home these events had taken place, it must have been very difficult. Their love and support will never be forgotten.

We took Claire's body home for the funeral, so that our family and friends could say goodbye and share in thanksgiving for her life. The results of the post-mortem showed that Claire had died from bronchopneumonia. The pathologist concluded that in view of the problems she had, her life had been much longer than he would have expected.

Dr Janet agreed to our request to speak about Claire during the funeral service. Her words were to have a far-reaching effect. This is what she said:

A funeral is a time of taking stock. Claire's funeral is a time for giving thanks for her and taking stock of what her life said to us. The passage that we have just read (Mark 10:13–16) is such an appropriate reading, as no doubt some of the parents who brought their children to Jesus had handicapped children whom they hoped that he would heal. Yet disciples tried to drive them back, because they thought that the Lord would not be interested in them. This is still true of many people's attitude towards handicapped children as they see without perceiving, judging by externals only. Claire's handicapped body was just the house that she lived in, but the light shone out through her windows, with love and laughter. Those of us who watched her impact on her family saw how powerful this was and how loving she was. So many able-bodied people are unable to love others properly and if handicapped children like Claire, James and others contribute nothing else to society than this, surely to put in more love means that their lives have been worth while? As the Gospel reading said, so it was true of Claire, that the Lord had laid his hands upon her and blessed her. Where love is, there God is also.

The pearl.

We cannot deny the fact of pain. There is disappointment and even dismay when a child is found to be handicapped. Yet the oyster reminds us that pain can be transformed into something of great value: the little piece of grit, so irritating and distressing, is slowly covered and changed into the pearl. A piece of grit in human tissue may cause an abscess and it remains true that for some, the hurt of handicap continues as a throbbing and resented pain. We do not know the oyster's secret, but I believe that for us it is the love of God which, when allowed, lubricates the hurting places in our spirits and changes them so wonderfully. This is not to say that God designs handicapped children, but when one comes he bestows special grace to help in time of need.

There will still be those who ask, 'Why?' 'If God is all powerful, why does he allow suffering?' It is a comfort to remember that, even on the cross, the Lord Jesus himself cried, 'Why?' Yet the answer slowly unfolded. In a way that we cannot fully understand, the cross shows us God's own great suffering as he came in the person of Christ to bridge the gap which had arisen as humanity put love of self before love of God. We are told that another name for Christ is the 'pearl of great price', formed as he lovingly, but painfully, took the world's sin on himself. His rising from the dead is a picture of the new life he offers to each of us. All that we have to do is to reach out our hand to receive – but as his love was unconditional, so should be our response. If we are to know the full extent of his love in our lives, the entry fee is nothing, but the annual subscription is everything. Trusting him through thick and thin is how we find that his love never fails and that he can change grit into glory. Whether believers or not, this is what we have seen happening through Claire and the life and love achieved through her within her family.

The candle.

She was well named Claire, speaking of clarity and purity. It seemed that she shone 'with a pure, clear light, like a little candle burning in the night'. The love coming from Claire brightened her own night of disability, the night of her family's disappointment and the night of other people's doubts that a handicapped life was not worth having. The effect of one candle power depends greatly on the darkness around it and Claire's life and light were used to dispel clouds of misunderstanding and prejudice. Our forebears used to use candles as their main form of lighting; nowadays we have neon lights and even brighter lights instead. Yet there is one thing that a candle can do that no other light is able to do and that is that it can light another candle. So today, as we reflect on what the life of this little girl said to us, may our lives begin to shine with the love and light of the God who worked through her.

In my own reading, on the morning of this service, in the last chapter of the Bible I read 'and there shall be no night there; and they need no candle, neither light of the sun; for the Lord God giveth them light' (Rev 22:5). This is now true for Claire. May she lead the rest of us, with God's help, to get our own priorities straighter.

The final reading sums up for us many of these thoughts: 'To know the love of Christ which surpasses knowledge' (Eph 3:14–19).

Claire and James brought the love of God into our lives – that is the greatest gift that one person can give another. We knew her death was inevitable, yet nothing could prepare us for life without her – and without Jimmy too. It was close to unbearable.

For nearly nine years we had been a family; now there was a gaping hole, with emotions in its depths that I cannot find the words to describe. There were long, desperate times.

The many letters we received reminded us that we were not alone. People wrote to tell us that their lives had been enriched through knowing Claire. Others wrote, remembering the happy, funny times. Some friends of ours were separated and on the point of divorce when Claire died. They both came to the funeral and wrote afterwards: 'We had a long talk after Claire's funeral service today. We are going to try again, to make our marriage work.'

Claire's contribution to the materialistic society into which she was born was nil in financial terms. But if there was some way to measure the spiritual wealth she brought to so many people, then her contribution can be seen quite differently. This is so, not just for Claire and Jimmy, but for many other severely handicapped people too. I do not think that God chooses for children to be handicapped, or for them to die. But what he does do is to give in abundance the special help we need to deal with these tragedies, and through suffering, reach a new dimension. The tragedy evolves into something pure and true, born of the power of God.

We live in a world where it is vitally important to have clever, well-qualified people who can contribute to the economy; obviously it is necessary for our survival. But at the same time it is equally vital that we nourish our spirituality. Do we really want to live in a society that puts more emphasis on financial concerns than on compassion, kindness and caring for our fellow men and women? We must be able to strike a balance.

As I finish the story of Claire and Jimmy, it is 1995, ten years since Jimmy's death and seven since Claire's. Yet time is an enigma; it could have happened yesterday, or a hundred years ago. I still think about them both many times each day. We have learned to live with their absence. The once permanent, raw grief now appears less often, replaced by smiling memories and the knowledge that the love we all shared will never die. It is not the end.

In the year after Claire died, Dick and I were thrilled to be expecting our third child. We put our faith and trust in God, knowing that whatever happened we would dearly love this new baby, who was due on 28th May 1989, Claire's birthday.

This brings us full circle, to the first paragraph of this book. The little girl running towards me in the sunshine is Alice, Claire and Jimmy's little sister. She is beautiful and bright; a gift from God.

'And my cup overflows' (Ps 23:5).